C0-ATC-189

# Jesus is Lord

# Jesus is Lord

A study in the unity of confessing
Jesus as Lord and Saviour
in the New Testament

## T. ALAN CHRISOPE

EVANGELICAL PRESS

EVANGELICAL PRESS
16/18 High Street, Welwyn, Hertfordshire AL6 9EQ, England

© Evangelical Press 1982
*First published 1982*

ISBN 0 85234—160-1

All Scripture quotations are from the New American Standard Bible unless clearly the author's own translation or otherwise designated.

Typeset in Great Britain by Inset, Hertford

Printed in the U.S.A.

To

# REDEEMER BAPTIST CHURCH

Columbus, Nebraska

# Contents

# Foreword

'Jesus is Lord' is the most fundamental and basic confession of the New Testament church. With words such as these in Romans 10:9, 10 the apostle Paul describes the basic confession which results in salvation.

Some within the Christian community today would argue that the confession of Jesus as Lord is a later stage of Christian growth which follows after and is distinct from the earlier confession of Jesus as Saviour.

Recognizing that Christians grow in their awareness of and submission to the lordship of Jesus, Pastor Chrisope seeks to point the way out of this apparent conflict between experience on the one hand and the claims of the New Testament on the other, while at the same time dealing with the more fundamental question of the nature of Jesus' lordship and its relationship to man's salvation.

By careful and faithful attention to the passages of the New Testament, Mr Chrisope unfolds the meaning and significance of Jesus' lordship, especially for man and his salvation. The mediatorial lordship of Jesus, that is the lordship resultant upon the redemptive work and exaltation of the incarnate Lord, is given its full New Testament significance without ignoring or minimizing the lordship intrinsic to the Son of God as the second Person of the Trinity. With great clarity and readability, the author not only surveys the biblical evidence but also with courtesy and fairness deals with opposing viewpoints in the light of that evidence.

At the end of the book, the reader has acquired an answer to the question: 'In becoming a Christian, is one biblically required to acknowledge Jesus Christ as Lord?' and also an informed awareness of what that means both for the one who shares the gospel and for the one who receives it.

I heartily commend this Master's thesis by my former student to the Christian community.

*George W. Knight, III,*
*Professor of New Testament,*
*Covenant Theological Seminary,*
*St Louis, Missouri, U.S.A.*

# Preface

This volume is offered to the Christian public, not as a final solution to the problem which it addresses, but as a contribution to the ongoing discussion. My modest hope is that it will help to clarify and contribute to the resolution of that question which is its central issue: 'What is the proper place of the lordship of Jesus Christ in the Christian confession?' Its author recognizes that he himself is not above the need for correction and further instruction; all such which is offered in a Christian spirit will be welcomed.

My thanks are due to Dr George W. Knight, III, of Covenant Theological Seminary in St Louis, for his instruction and example in the study of the New Testament and its theology, for his encouragement and wise counsel during the course of this writing project, and for the gracious foreword which he kindly contributed to this volume.

Special thanks are due also to Dr Robert L. Reymond (also of Covenant Seminary), without whose encouragement this book would not have been written; to my wife Linda, for her help, encouragement and patience during my preoccupation with this project over a period of many months; and to the good people of Redeemer Baptist Church in Columbus, Nebraska, who for seven years have provided me with the opportunity to be engaged in the ministry of the Word, and who endured most of the contents of this volume in a lengthy series of studies.

Grateful appreciation must also be expressed to Evangelical Press for their patience and understanding in dealing with a fledgling author; and to the Banner of Truth Trust for permission to quote the extended passage which constitutes the appendix to this volume.

I commit this book into the hands of our Sovereign God to use as He sees fit. *Soli Deo Gloria.*

*T. Alan Chrisope*

# Introduction

In September 1959 there appeared in *Eternity* magazine a written debate between Everett F. Harrison and John R. W. Stott. The debate was entitled 'Must Christ Be Lord To Be Saviour?'; Harrison argued for a negative answer to that question while Stott advocated a positive response.[1] The opinion of the editors on this question was not made clear, but it appears that they may have favoured the affirmative answer, for they placed Harrison's article first and allowed Stott to reply to it in a lengthier and more detailed response.

The issue was not resolved by the *Eternity* debate, for ten years later Charles Caldwell Ryrie published a book bearing the title *Balancing the Christian Life*, which included a chapter also entitled 'Must Christ be Lord to be Saviour?'[2] Ryrie joins Harrison in answering the question in the negative, though he does so much more pointedly. He quotes Stott along with J. I. Packer and Arthur W. Pink as examples of those who would offer an affirmative answer to the question, and then brings the issue very sharply into focus by affirming that these two answers cannot both be correct, they 'cannot both be the gospel; therefore one of them is a false gospel and comes under the curse of perverting the gospel or preaching another gospel (Gal. 1:6—9), and this is a very serious matter.'[3] Ryrie has little difficulty in making it clear which of these positions he regards as the 'false gospel'.

Then in 1976 Harrison again speaks to the issue in his contribution on Romans in *The Expositor's Bible Commentary.* He writes concerning Romans 10:9—10 as follows: 'Paul's statement in vv. 9—10 is misunderstood when it is made to support the claim that one cannot be saved unless he makes Jesus the Lord of his life by a personal commitment . . . Paul is speaking of the objective lordship of Christ.'[4]

These varied items make it clear that there is considerable theological tension concerning the question at issue. The question is this: 'In becoming a Christian, is one biblically required to acknowledge Jesus Christ as Lord? Or is that acknowledgement something which can be relegated to a later point in the Christian life?' The debate is not an inconsequential one for, as Ryrie has observed, it is nothing less than the definition of the gospel which is at stake.

Neither is the question without its practical ramifications. The Christian community's commitment to one or the other of these positions cannot but manifest itself daily in popular theology and in practical Christian living, as well as in preaching and evangelism. The issue intrudes itself into the life of the church at a most vital level. This is illustrated by an article in the February 1978 issue of the *Baptist Herald,* a denominational periodical published by the fellowship to which the present writer belongs. The article is entitled 'Is Jesus Christ the Lord of Your Life?' and consists primarily of a report on the activities of a musical evangelistic team. The team's programme and the article have the laudable intention of encouraging Christians to live in practical observance of Christ's lordship. But the theological basis for the approach taken is that 'there is indeed a difference between having Jesus as Saviour and having Him as Lord and controller of our lives'.[5] Because of this difference, the Christian who has received Jesus as Saviour is to be further encouraged to 'make Jesus Lord' of his life.

Admittedly such teaching is popular, but is it true? The real question is 'Is it biblical?' The present writer believes not; it is the thesis of this study that, in biblical terms, there is no difference between having Jesus Christ as Saviour and having Him as Lord; that the two concepts are regarded as equivalent in the New Testament. This will be demonstrated by first examining the meaning of *kyrios,* the Greek word which is translated 'lord' in the New Testament (Chapter 1). Our attention will then be focused on the theological significance of 'lordship' as it is attributed to Jesus following His resurrection (Chapter 2). Thirdly, the proclamation and confession that 'Jesus is Lord' will be examined as to its place and meaning in the New Testament, and objections to the interpretation which is offered here will be dealt with (Chapter 3). Finally, some practical considerations will be set forth in the form of questions concerning our handling of the gospel and some suggested correctives which are broadly applicable to the evangelical Christian community (Chapter 4).

This study has no merely polemical interest, but is the product of pastoral experience and concern. It deals with no light matters, but rather with the nature of the gospel of the eternal God and with man's appropriate response to that divine Word. Come, let us reason together.

# 1

# The meaning of the title 'Lord' (*kyrios*)

The foundation for a study of the lordship of Jesus Christ and its implications must be laid in an examination of the meaning and use of the Greek word *kyrios,* the word which is commonly translated 'Lord' when applied to Jesus in the New Testament.[1]

The noun *ho kyrios* is the substantive form of the adjective *kyrios,* which when used of persons means 'having power or authority over', and which in turn derives from another noun, *to kyros,* meaning 'supreme power, authority'.[2] The idea of legitimacy attaches to the authority or power represented by *kyrios* (both the adjective and the noun) so that it refers to an authority which lawfully, validly and legitimately belongs to the one who possesses it. '*Kyrios* always contains the idea of legality and authority,'[3] and thus sometimes stands in contrast to *despotēs* (also meaning 'master' or 'lord'), which may carry overtones of high-handedness. *Despotēs* speaks of the possession or exercise of power in fact, while *kyrios* emphasizes the legitimacy and authority of the power exercised. The root idea of *kyrios* is thus legitimate authority, a fact which will be borne out by the following brief survey of the ancient use of the word. We may conveniently divide our treatment historically, according to classical usage (including Hellenistic), Old Testament usage (in the Septuagint) and New Testament usage.

## The classical usage of *kyrios*

In classical usage, *ho kyrios* first appears with a fixed sense in the early fourth century B.C., where it has two distinct meanings: 'the lawful owner of a slave', and 'the legal guardian of a wife or girl'; both reflect the idea of 'one who has full authority'.[4] The word had only limited use in the Attic (literary) dialect, but there it derived from the adjective 'a restriction to legitimate power of disposal which is never wholly lost in the *koine* ['common' dialect]'.[5] In the *koine*, *kyrios* is often used interchangeably with *despotēs*, but a distinction may still be discerned: '*Kyrios* is the one who can dispose of something or someone, *despotēs* the one who owns something or someone.'[6] As the New Testament era nears, the more *kyrios* tends to displace *despotēs*; it is the more flattering term.

In the realm of religion, although the term *kyrios* is sometimes applied to the gods, the Greeks generally did not regard their gods as possessing lordship, except perhaps in limited spheres. The reason is that the Greek gods were not personal creator-gods, and thus evoked no corresponding human response of submission. The gods were, like men, subject to fate, not the lords of fate. 'At root, man has no personal responsibility towards these gods, nor can they personally encounter man with punishments'; gods and men 'are organically related members of one reality, and their mutual relation cannot be described in terms of *kyrios* and *doulos* ['lord' and 'slave'] '.[7]

In the East, however, the religious situation was different. For the inhabitants of Egypt, Syria and Asia Minor 'the gods are the lords of reality. Destiny is in their hands.'[8] They are creator-gods, they can intervene in the world and in human affairs, and man is responsible to them. 'They are the lords of destiny and the lords of men,'[9] and are treated as such by their human subjects. This basic difference between Greece and the East paved the way for a broader application of *kyrios* to the gods during the Hellenistic period.

As the use of the Greek language spread over the Mediterranean world during the Hellenistic period (from about 323 B.C. to the New Testament era), the application of *kyrios* to the gods became relatively more prevalent in the East than it was in Greece, although Foerster remarks that '*kyrios* never became widespread as a predicate of the gods',[10] and he finds no instance of it (except for *kyrios* with the genitive, 'lord of . . .') prior to the first century B.C. Its local use in various places 'corresponded to native, non-Greek usage'[11] — that is, it simply reflected the local idiom.

There are two features of this application of *kyrios* to the gods which are of special interest to our present investigation. In the first place, *kyrios* 'is particularly used in expression of a personal relationship of man to the deity . . . and as a correlate of *doulos* inasmuch as the man concerned describes as *kyrios* the god under whose orders he stands'.[12] Secondly, the gods to whom *kyrios* is most commonly applied are those in whom the attribute of 'dominion over nature and destiny is most impressively present'.[13] Thus there is present in this usage the idea of the power and authority of the god who is termed *kyrios,* as well as the implication of a personal relationship involving submission of the worshipper to his god.

The attributes of power and authority also attach to positions of rulership in the human political sphere, and *kyrios* was eventually applied to them as well. This is observable in the first centuries B.C. and A.D., as political rulers both in the East and in Rome are termed *kyrios* (for example, the Roman emperors Augustus, Caligula, Nero and Domitian; the Palestinian rulers Herod the Great, Agrippa I and Agrippa II; and the Queen of Upper Egypt).[14] It is a matter of dispute whether this title implied the divinity of the ruler, a question which lies beyond the scope of the present discussion.[15] It is sufficient for our purpose to note that *kyrios* was used of those who in the human sphere occupied positions of legitimate authority and power.

## The Old Testament usage of *kyrios*

In the Septuagint *kyrios* occurs over 9,000 times. Three major aspects of its occurrence are of particular interest for the present discussion. First, *kyrios* is used to translate various Hebrew and Aramaic words which refer to men. The most common of these is *adōn* (lord), which is often used as a polite form of address (Gen. 19:2; 32:4), but which perhaps also often implies the superior position of the one addressed or referred to (e.g., when used of kings and other rulers, Gen. 47:25;

throughout 2 Sam., 1 Kings 1, etc.). Sometimes *adōn* (and thus *kyrios*) refers directly to a position of rulership (Gen. 45:8, 9; Ps. 105:21). *Kyrios* also translates several other words which refer to positions of authority: *gebir,* 'master' (Gen. 27:29, 37); *baal,* 'owner' (Judg. 19:22, 23); and the Aramaic *shallit,* 'ruler' (Dan. 4:17, Theodotion's version [4:14 in Aramaic] ); and *mara,* 'lord', used both of God (Dan. 2: 47; 5:23, Theodotion) and men (Dan. 4:19, 24, Theodotion [4:16, 21 in Aramaic]).

Second, *kyrios* is used many times to translate *adōn* when the latter refers to God. It is used alone (Gen. 18: 27; Ps. 113 [114, Heb.]:7) and in combination with other titles and names of God (Isa. 28:22; Amos 9:5; Zeph. 1:9). As a name for God, *kyrios* is a strict translation of the Hebrew only in such cases where it represents *adōn.* The two words are roughly equivalent in that both mean 'lord', implying rightful authority and power.

In the third place, *kyrios* is used most often in the Septuagint (some 6,156 times) to represent *YHWH,* the proper name of God. In these instances, Bietenhard points out, it is not a strict translation but 'an interpretative circumlocution'; it stands for 'all that the Hebrew text implied by the divine name', namely, that 'Yahweh is Creator and Lord of the whole universe' and 'the God of Israel, His covenant people'. Further, 'By choosing *kyrios* for Yahweh the LXX Greek text also emphasized the idea of legal authority. Because Yahweh saved his people from Egypt and chose them as his possession, he is the legitimate Lord of Israel. As Creator of the world he is also its legitimate Lord with unlimited control over it.'[16]

It is thus evident that the use of *kyrios* in the Septuagint is consistently coloured by the implication of legitimate power and authority, whether the term is applied to God or to men.

## The New Testament usage of *kyrios*

In the New Testament there are two levels of common usage of *kyrios*, the secular and the religious, both of which continue to maintain the idea of legitimate power and authority, which was originally inherent in the word.

In secular usage *kyrios* can mean the 'owner' of something, for example, a vineyard (Matt. 20:8), a house (Mark 13:35), or a colt (Luke 19:33). This meaning passes easily into that of 'lord' or 'master', 'one who has full control of something',[17] for instance, the harvest (Matt. 9:38) or the sabbath (Mark 2:28) — though in fact both these references have religious significance, since they apply to God and to Jesus respectively. *Kyrios* can also denote the owner or master of a slave or servant (*doulos* — as in John 13:16, Matt. 10:24; 18:31; Eph. 6:5 and several other New Testament passages). The vocative form *kyrie* is commonly used by slaves in addressing their masters (Matt. 13:27; 25:20, 22, 24; Luke 14:22). *Kyrios* is used to designate a person of high or superior position, such as a husband in contrast to his wife (1 Peter 3:6), a father (Matt. 21:29—30, various readings), or a civil official (Matt. 27:63). This usage shades into *kyrie* as a form of polite address, equivalent to the English 'sir'. It is used in addressing Jesus as well as others (Matt. 25:

21

11; John 4:11; 12:21; 20:15; Acts 16:30).

*Kyrios* is more commonly used in the New Testament, however, in a religious sense. It often refers to God, either as used by the New Testament writers directly (Luke 1:6, 28) or, as is frequently the case, in quotations from the Old Testament (Mark 12:36; Acts 3:22; Rom. 9:28—29). This use of *kyrios* is simply a continuation of Septuagint usage, and is intended to imply all that was meant by the Hebrew *YHWH*.

But it is in reference to Jesus that *kyrios* finds its most distinctive use in the New Testament. The term is applied to Him throughout the book, but we may approach the matter historically by dividing the career of Jesus into two periods — that before His resurrection, and that after it. This is not an arbitrary division, nor one of mere convenience, for it has considerable theological significance. It is during the period following Jesus' resurrection that *kyrios* becomes, as Geerhardus Vos put it, the 'specific designation of the exalted Saviour'.[18] It is thus with this period, and with the application of *kyrios* to the exalted Jesus, that the present study is primarily concerned. But neither can the earlier period be ignored, for with respect to the use of *kyrios* in reference to Jesus, there seems to be a good deal of continuity between the two. That is, during the earthly life of Jesus, *kyrios* was applied to Him in such a way as to imply recognition of His divine person and Messianic office.

A demonstration of this would require a full treatment of the use of *kyrios* in the Gospels, which is beyond the scope of the present study. A brief survey must suffice to indicate the pertinent lines of thought. *Kyrios* is applied to Jesus in three ways in the Gospel accounts. First, the Gospel writers themselves (as distinct from personages within the Gospels) use *kyrios* of Jesus, either directly in the narrative (Luke 7:13 and often in Luke; seldom in John; hardly at all in Matthew and Mark) or in Old Testament quotations (probably Mark 1:3). Second, persons within the narrative speak of Jesus as 'Lord' or 'the Lord' (Luke 1:43; 19:34), including Jesus Himself, directly (Luke 6:5; 19:31) and in parables (Mark 13:35). Third, persons in the narrative address Jesus as 'Lord' (Matt. 8:2, 25, etc.). Geerhardus Vos draws the following conclusions concerning these three modes of usage: (i) The Gospel writers themselves attach 'a higher and richer significance to the name *kyrios* beginning with the resurrection',[19] as indicated by their infrequent use of that title before the resurrection and their more frequent use of it afterwards. (ii) When persons within the Gospel narrative refer to Jesus as a third person using *kyrios* ('the Lord' etc.), there occurs in many cases 'a real anticipation of the subsequent usage',[20] that is, as a Christological title (Luke 1:43; 2:11; 6:5 and parallels; 19:31 and parallels, 20:41—44 and parallels). (iii) When the vocative *kyrie* is used in addressing Jesus, it is often 'a real precursor of the standard designation of the Saviour from the apostolic age onwards . . . It recognizes His Messianic character and, at times at least, His divine nature and dignity as reflected in His Messiahship' (Matt. 7:21; 8:21; 26:22; Luke 5:8).[21]

Vos's conclusions may be regarded as generally valid, although the evidence in support of the first point does not seem to be as strong as he supposes. The other two, however, are based on sounder evidence, and indicate that *kyrios* as applied to Jesus in the Gospels to a large degree anticipates the usage that later became common among Christians.

Vos goes on to make two further observations which have a bearing on our present study. The first is that the evidence for the lordship of Jesus in the Gospels is not limited to the use of particular words (e.g. *kyrios*). That evidence extends rather to the 'general structure of the relation of the disciples to Jesus in the record . . . The absolute things asked of the disciples, the unqualified duty to follow – to forsake all others for Jesus' sake, including even the dearest of earthly relationships . . . – all this demands for its ultimate ground His unique Lordship as recognized even at that time.'[22] Such a relationship manifests the essence of lordship, and as we shall have opportunity to observe later, is qualitatively no different from that which obtains between Jesus and believers following His exaltation.

Second, Vos notes that 'the presence of one stable element from beginning to end marks the continuity in the history of the conception' of Jesus' lordship in the New Testament, that is, 'the element of authoritative ownership,'[23] which serves as the ground for the absolute demands made on the disciples of Jesus. This idea is present both before and after the resurrection and serves to demonstrate the basic meaning of divine lordship in the New Testament, particularly as exercised by Jesus.

As was noted above, it is after the resurrection that *kyrios* becomes the distinctive designation of Jesus as the *exalted* Saviour. We turn now to a consideration of His exaltation and the significance of *kyrios* as applied to Him in His exalted state throughout the rest of the New Testament.

# 2
# The mediatorial lordship of Jesus Christ

In this chapter we are concerned to examine several representative New Testament passages which set forth the fact of the exaltation of Christ and its implications. Most prominent among these are Philippians 2:9—11, Acts 2:36 and Romans 1:3—4, all of which deal primarily with the basic fact of Jesus' exaltation, although they also give intimations of the authority belonging to Him as exalted Lord. This latter topic will be dealt with in its own right as we give attention to Matthew 28: 18—20, Ephesians 1:20—23 and Romans 14:9, passages which treat more specifically of the nature of the authority which Jesus possesses in His exaltation.

The name of this aspect of Christian theology — 'the exaltation of Christ' — is derived from the word 'exalt', a term which occurs in only one of the six passages metioned above (Phil. 2:9—11). This passage contains a compound form of the Greek word *hypsoō*, which means 'lift up' or 'raise high',[1] and which occurs in its simple form in Acts 2:33 and 5:31. In both of these latter passages (which are specimens of Peter's preaching) *hypsoō* refers to the elevation of Jesus after His resurrection to a position of supreme authority at the right hand of God.[2] Paul in Philippians 2:9 seems to use the term (in its compound form, *hyperhypsoō*, 'highly exalt') in a somewhat broader sense, to denote the whole complex of redemptive events which followed upon the death of Jesus, including His resurrection, ascension and seating at the right hand of God. It is these events, then, which form the subject of the present chapter. While not all the passages which will be examined contain the term 'exalt', they do refer to the event itself, and thus claim our attention.

The remaining occurrences of *hypsoō* in the New Testament are the three times it is found in the Gospel of John. On all three occasions (John 3:14; 8:28; 12:32) it is found on the lips of Jesus, and in each case it refers primarily to His death by crucifixion. Many interpreters believe that a double meaning is intended in these instances and that the exaltation to heaven is also in view.[3] While this usage is certainly interesting in its own right, our concern here will be with the more explicit passages of the New Testament.

### The exaltation of Jesus as Lord

In the New Testament the exaltation of Jesus is inseparably connected with that position of lordship into which He was installed upon being exalted — in short, being exalted meant being made mediatorial Lord. We will first examine those New Testament passages which directly connect exaltation and lordship; then there will follow a section dealing with the nature of Jesus' authority as Lord. All of this will be found to have ramifications for the preaching of the gospel and the confession which it elicits, the subject of the next chapter.

*Philippians 2:9–11.* The passage in which the exaltation of Jesus is most closely linked with the title 'Lord' is Philippians 2:9–11. This passage and its context, beginning with verse 5, has given rise to a great variety of interpretations, especially in recent decades.[4] But the full scope of this debate need not concern us now; for as George Eldon Ladd has remarked, 'One fact is clear in all interpretations of the passage: because of his self-emptying and obedience unto death, something new has been bestowed upon him [Jesus] — a new name indicating a new role and status: *kyrios.*'[5] Ladd's remark anticipates the conclusion of our present investigation; we proceed now to a few pertinent observations on the details of the text.

*1.* The exaltation of Jesus is represented as something which He experienced in His incarnate state; it occurs subsequent to and as a consequence of His obedience unto death (v. 8). The implications of this fact are not always appreciated; if they were, there would be less confusion over the question of how Jesus, if He existed previously in the form of God (v. 6), could now be exalted. Confusion over this point can be found, however, among scholars as diverse in outlook as E. Käsemann[6] and Lewis Sperry Chafer.[7] It was not, of course, with respect to God the Son, conceived purely as Deity, that the exaltation took place, but with respect to Jesus of Nazareth, the God-man, the Son of God incarnate. The entire incarnate existence of Jesus previous to His exaltation had been one of humiliation (vv. 6—8); but now, He who once willingly humbled Himself has been gloriously exalted.

2. The exaltation of Jesus was accomplished in the closest connection with the bestowal on Him of the supreme name (v. 9). Upon His exaltation, Jesus was 'freely given'[8] (*echarisato*, aorist) by God 'the name which is above every name', a name which we may thus assume (without necessarily looking beyond v. 9) to be expressive of supremacy and of the highest authority. In His exaltation and in the bestowal of the name which He received, Jesus was inaugurated into a new and distinct phase of His redemptive career. He entered into a status that He had not known before *as the God-man:* previously, He was the God-man in humility; now He is the God-man in exaltation — and He is given a name commensurate with His new status.

3. The name which Jesus received at the time of His exaltation, that name which both constitutes and expresses His exaltation, is the title 'Lord' (*kyrios*, v. 11). R. P. Martin comments, 'As to the content of the name which is bestowed, there is now general agreement that this is to be understood in terms of *Kyrios.*'[9] There are several reasons for making this identification: (i) Verse 9 leads us to expect *the* pre-eminent name. 'The repetition of the definite article in verse 9c [*to onoma to hyper pan onoma*] prepares us for a declaration of the very name of God Himself,'[10] which *kyrios* in fact is, in common Septuagint and New Testament usage. (ii) This identification fits well with the flow of the passage. J. A. Motyer has noted that the movement in verses 9—11 is from the bestowal of 'the name' in verse 9 straight through to 'the universal confession

that "Jesus Christ is Lord" ' in verse 11.[11] The passage begins with 'the name' and climaxes with *kyrios.* The identification of the two is natural. (iii) In verses 10—11, where the affinities with Isaiah 45:23 are too strong to ignore (compare with the Septuagint), the exalted Jesus occupies the place assigned to God in the Old Testament text. If divine honour is bestowed on Jesus, as this use of the Isaiah passage implies (a passage which, it should be noted, is strongly mono-theistic in tone), then it is not unreasonable that the divine name should also be given Him — which is exactly what occurs when the name *kyrios* is applied to Jesus (v. 11). (iv) No other name so admirably as *kyrios* fits the description in verse 9. 'Jesus' was given in infancy, not at the exaltation (and, as J. B. Lightfoot notes, verse 10 reads, 'at the name *of* Jesus,' not 'at the name Jesus'[12]). 'Christ' is the title of an office which He exercised well before this exaltation. Other suggested names are no more suitable than these. Even Lightfoot, who prefers to take 'name' as 'not meaning a definite appellation but denoting office, rank, dignity,' must admit that 'if St Paul were refer-ring to any one term, *kyrios* would best explain the reference'.[13] But there is no compelling reason to divorce the office from the appellation, especially when the latter is provided by the passage itself.

4. The bestowal of the name 'Lord' (*kyrios*) upon Jesus indicates His installation as supreme sovereign of the universe. This is demonstrated by the fact that every knee shall bow and every tongue confess His lordship (vv. 10—11), as well as by the concept and content of the 'name' itself. In biblical usage 'name'

is commonly a revelation of the character of the one named;[14] thus 'the name of *Kyrios* involves divine equality, for it authorizes Jesus to act in the capacity of God *vis-a-vis* the world, to receive the rightful obeisance of all created powers and to share the throne of the universe'.[15] The God-man, Christ Jesus, is granted (under the Father) all the rights and prerogatives of God in the governance of the universe, and as verses 10—11 indicate, all due acknowledgement will be made of that fact by those over whom His rule is established.

5.   It is by means of the acknowledgement of the lordship of Jesus that God the Father is glorified (v. 11). This verse serves as an indicator of one of the ultimate purposes of God: that Jesus should be acclaimed as Lord by all the personal beings of the universe, which acclamation will redound to the glory of God the Father Himself. Since this acclamation will, at least on the part of those beings who are hostile to God, be made dutifully rather than willingly, the verb 'confess' (*exomologeō*) should be understood to indicate an acknowledgement of fact rather than necessarily a confession arising from faith.[16] The confession is, for those hostile beings, the recognition of the undeniable fact of their subjection to Jesus as Lord, and stands in contrast to the humble and adoring submission rendered by believers.

While on the one hand the exaltation of Jesus to lordship is already an accomplished fact (note the aorists in v. 9: 'exalted ... bestowed'), and on the other hand the universal acknowledgement of that fact is yet future and awaits the powerful and glorious manifestation of His lordship,[17] the present implications of the point now under consideration ought not to be ignored. If it is through the specific confession that 'Jesus is Lord' that God will be glorified at the consummation, there is the strong presumption (in the light of the unity of God's redemptive purpose) that the same would hold true for the present age: that it is specifically through the Christian confession (rendered in advance of the consummation) that 'Jesus is Lord' (with the implication of personal submission to that lordship) that God has chosen to bring glory to Himself. There is in the New Testament a consistent pattern of teaching which confirms this supposition, as we shall see in the next chapter.

Until now we have used without explanation (for example, in the title of this chapter) the term 'mediatorial' with reference to that lordship which Jesus exercises since His exaltation. Since this term defines a helpful theological distinction, and since its meaning is well illustrated by Philippians 2:9—11, perhaps this would be an appropriate point at which to expand upon it.

The term 'mediatorial' refers in general to the work accomplished by the Son of God in His various offices (Prophet, Priest and King) while in His incarnate state, as distinct from His pre-incarnate existence.[18] 'Mediatorial' is applied to the lordship which Christ presently exercises in order to distinguish it from that eternal dominion which He possesses as God the Son. The latter is His by inherent right, while the former, as defined by Louis Berkhof, 'is a conferred and economical kingship, exercised by Christ, not merely in His divine nature, but as *Theanthropos* (the God-man) . . . [It] is not a kingship that was Christ's by original right, but one with which He is invested.'[19]

The title 'mediator' is applied to Christ four times in the New Testament (1 Tim. 2:5; Heb. 8:6; 9:15; 12:24) and always in connection with the redeeming work accomplished by Him in His incarnate state. The three passages in Hebrews designate Christ as the mediator of the New Covenant (mentioned in the closest connection with His death; see especially Heb. 9:15 and 12:24), while 1 Timothy 2:5 declares Him to be the 'one mediator between God and men', identified emphatically as 'the *man* Christ Jesus' (emphasis mine).

The implications of mediatorship with respect to Jesus are consistent with the New Testament data: (i) His position as mediator is an office which He fills in the unity of His 'entire theanthropic person',[20] not just His divine or human nature. It is 'the man Christ Jesus' that is exalted to lordship. (ii) His mediatorship involves an economic — not essential — subordination to God the Father: it is in the Father's behalf that He reigns as King. 'Christ is Lord over all, but Lord as Servant of Jehovah. He reigns, but as the representative of God . . . He sways a universal sceptre, but only in the name of God and according to His will.'[21] It is perhaps in this connection that 1 Corinthians 15:24—28 should be understood, a passage which speaks of the subjection of Christ to God the Father. (iii) With regard to the duration of His mediatorial work, including His kingship or lordship, there is disagreement, even among Reformed writers. W. G. T. Shedd contends that 'there will not always be a mediatorial work going on'[22] (1 Cor. 15:24—28 is often appealed to in this connection). On the other hand, Herman Hoeksema asserts that 'the Word of God emphasizes everywhere that Christ's office is without end; and that His dominion is an ever-lasting dominion, that He must reign forever, that He is a priest forever after the order of Melchisedec'.[23] Hoeksema's position would seem to have the strong (and perhaps decisive) support of Psalm 110, to which he alludes in the quotation above. 'The Lord has sworn and will not change His mind, "Thou art a priest forever according to the order of Melchizedek" ' (Ps. 110:4). Hebrews 5:6, 10 and 6:20—8:1 make it clear that the reference in Psalm 110 is to Christ; and thus it would appear that His office of Priest-King (after the pattern of Melchizedek) is an everlasting one (for the con-junction of both offices in Christ, see Heb. 8:1).

The answer to this last question is not crucial to the present discussion. The overriding point is that it is within the context of mediatorship as outlined above that the exaltation of Jesus to lordship is to be under-stood; He is God's duly appointed kingly representative, the God-man who reigns in God's behalf over the universe.

*Acts 2:36.* Acts 2:36 is another passage of funda-mental importance for establishing the New Testament teaching on the lordship of Jesus. The occasion is that of Peter's address on the day of Pentecost, and it thus places us at a very early point in the developing theo-logy of the young church.

Peter's affirmation is that 'God has made Him both Lord and Christ — this Jesus whom you crucified.' Concerning this declaration and the context in which it is made, a few relevant observations may be noted (dealing first with the title 'Lord' and then with the more problematic title — in this context — 'Christ').

*1.* Peter affirms that Jesus was 'made' Lord, indicating a new and distinctive phase of Messiah's career. The verb *poieō*, used in this particular construction, means 'make someone (into) something,'[24] that is, in this instance, Jesus was made to be Lord. As Joseph Addison Alexander has pointed out, *poieō* 'is never a mere synonym of *showed, declared*',[25] and thus the meaning cannot be weakened to indicate the mere declaration or demonstration of Jesus' lordship, but must refer to His actual installation into the office of 'Lord'. The action of God mentioned in this verse relative to Jesus' lordship is, as Alexander contends, not a 'declaratory act' but a 'constituting act'.[26]

*2.* The term 'Lord', as used in Acts 2:36, refers not to Jesus' essential deity but to the office of sovereign authority into which He was installed at his exaltation. Alexander again has an appropriate comment: '*Lord* cannot mean a divine person . . . for the Father did not make the Son to be God, but must mean a mediatorial sovereign.'[27] Once the meaning 'made' is acknowledged for *poieō,* then unless we are prepared to concede an adoptionist Christology here (which would contradict the rest of the New Testament), *kyrios* must be recognized as the title of the office into which Jesus was installed. The necessity for this understanding of *kyrios* is clearly demanded by the fact that God *made* Jesus to be such, which of course could not be predicated of His deity, which He already possessed and which is not, at any rate, an acquired quality. And this further underscores the need for the careful distinction that it was *as the God-man* that Jesus was exalted and invested with mediatorial lordship, a role which He had not previously enjoyed *as the God-man* and which stands in sharp contrast with His former (pre-resurrection) status of humility and servanthood.

3. The appointment of Jesus to lordship by God the Father occurred in conjunction with the resurrection and exaltation of Jesus mentioned in Acts 2:32—35. In fact, the two could almost be said to define each other: the exaltation of Jesus means His installation as Lord, and His installation as Lord is called His exaltation. The connecting link between these two concepts is supplied by the quotation from Psalm 110 in Acts 2:34—35. Falling as it does between the mention of Jesus' exaltation to God's right hand in verse 33, and His installation as Lord in verse 36, the citation of Psalm 110:1 brings both of these elements together in a single thought: David's Lord (*kyrios,* v. 34) is installed at God's right hand (v. 34) in a position of absolute authority (v. 35). This intimate connection of Jesus' present lordship with His resurrection and exaltation indicates that it was indeed a new phase of His ministry into which He entered when He was invested with authority as Lord. His mediatorial lordship is a bestowed position (as we have seen in Philippians 2:9—11) grounded in the redemption accomplished by His atoning death and brought about through His resurrection to glory and exaltation to the right hand of God. It is something which He is not said to possess before His resurrection.

4. Against this background the difficulties attending the interpretation of the title 'Christ' in verse 36

are not insuperable. The most plausible explanation is that offered by George Ladd: 'Peter means to say that Jesus has entered in upon a new stage of his messianic mission. He has now been enthroned as messianic King.' Ladd rejects the view that an adoptionist Christology is evidenced here (the view that 'Jesus *became* Messiah at His exaltation'), for other passages in Acts show that Peter knew otherwise: 'In the days of his flesh [Jesus] had been anointed (4:27; 10:38), and it was as the Messiah that he had suffered (3:18).' The meaning is, rather, that 'in his exaltation Jesus becomes the Messiah in a new sense: he has begun his messianic reign as the Davidic king'.[28] It is thus the regnal aspect of Jesus' messiahship that Peter refers to, as contrasted with His previous suffering and humiliation.

5. Verse 33 shows that Jesus was actively engaged in the exercise of His lordship, having bestowed on the infant church the promised Holy Spirit. Jesus, 'having been exalted to the right hand of God, and having received from the Father the promise of the Holy Spirit . . . has poured forth this which you both see and hear'. This shows that the lordship with which Jesus had been invested was such that it included His powerful and sovereign rule over His church. It was He who had 'received from the Father the promise of the Holy Spirit' and it was He who 'poured forth' that Spirit with its miraculous manifestations at Pentecost. He was indeed Lord — over the church as well as over the earth.

We have found then in Acts 2:36 a parallel to Philippians 2:9—11, teaching us that the exaltation which Jesus experienced subsequent to His resurrection consisted in His being granted, as the God-man, a position of supremacy and authority at God's right hand, a position to which is attached the title 'Lord', with all the rights and prerogatives which that title implies. This teaching is furthermore seen to be fundamental to the theology of the early New Testament church, climaxing as it does the first apostolic proclamation of the gospel after the descent of the Holy Spirit.

*Romans 1:4.* This is another passage which contributes significantly to our understanding of Jesus' exaltation and lordship, but concerning the interpretation of which there is considerable diversity of opinion. The major difficulties will be dealt with as we make a few observations on the text.

*1.* Paul here affirms[29] that the incarnate Son of God was, at a definite point in His career, appointed to a position of power which He had not before occupied.

The interpretation of the passage hinges on the meaning of the Greek word *horizō*, translated 'declared' by many English versions (KJV, NASB, NIV). The consistent meaning of the word in the New Testament, however, is not 'declare' but 'appoint', 'designate' or 'determine'. In other instances of its use in the New Testament, *horizō* refers to events foreordained by divine decree (Luke 22:22; Acts 2:23), to the divine determination of appointed times (Acts 17:26; Heb. 4:7) and to a human decision (Acts 11:29). In none of these cases does it bear the meaning 'declare'. And in two other instances where the object of the action of the verb is a person, in both cases it refers to Christ, and in both cases it clearly means 'appoint', 'ordain' or 'desig-

nate'. 'This is the One who has been *appointed* by God
as Judge of the living and the dead' (Acts 10:42). 'He
will judge the world in righteousness through a Man
whom He has *appointed*' (Acts 17:31). It is consistent,
therefore, with the meaning of the word and with New
Testament usage to translate Romans 1:4: 'Who was
*appointed* Son of God in power . . .'

The inclination of translators and interpreters to
assign to *horizō* the meaning 'declare' in this passage
stems from the understandable desire to avoid having
Paul (or the early church) appear to espouse an adoptionist Christology,[30] which would certainly be the case
if Jesus were said without further qualification to have
been appointed the Son of God. But there is a qualify-
ing element supplied by the passage itself, and when it
is properly understood, adoptionism is no longer the
necessary alternative. It was not simply to the position
of Son of God that Jesus was appointed, but (as the
translation suggested above indicates) to that of 'Son of
God in power'. As George Ladd notes, 'The key phrase
is "with power".'[31] Those two words make the essential distinction: they denote that mediatorial sovereignty with which Jesus was invested at His exaltation.
He was the Son of God already; He was appointed the
'Son of God in power' when God raised Him from the
dead and exalted Him to His own right hand. The phrase
'in power' is intended to contrast Jesus' present exalted
position with His former status of humility and weakness. Furthermore, ' "Son in power", ' Cullmann observes, 'is clearly synonymous with *Kyrios*.'[32] We have
in this verse an affirmation concerning Jesus' exaltation
to lordship.

This interpretation of Romans 1:4 is adopted by no less an exegete and theologian than the late John Murray, whose views are set forth most fully in his commentary on Romans[33] and are worthy of extensive quotation and careful attention. On the meaning of *horizō,* Murray writes, 'There is neither need nor warrant to resort to any other rendering than that provided by the other New Testament instances, namely, that Jesus was "appointed" or "constituted" Son of God with power and points therefore to an investiture which had an historical beginning parallel to the historical beginning mentioned in verse 3.'[34] With regard to the propriety of speaking of the 'appointment' of Jesus to this position of power, Murray notes that it is with respect to the Son of God *incarnate* that the assertion is made, and is altogether proper: 'The apostle is dealing with some particular event in the history of the Son of God incarnate by which he was *instated* in a position of sovereignty and invested with power, an event which in respect of investiture with power surpassed everything that could previously be ascribed to Him in His incarnate state.'[35] The entire passage (vv. 3—4) thus concerns the 'distinction drawn . . . between "two successive stages" of the historical process of which the Son of God became the subject' — the incarnation (v. 3) and the exaltation (v. 4).[36]

2. It may again be observed that this exaltation of Jesus was accomplished in connection with His resurrection. The instrumentality through which He was appointed Son-of-God-in-power was 'by the resurrection from the dead'. This serves to underline the fact that we are indeed dealing here with 'two success-

ive stages' in the ministry of Jesus — 'before the resurrection' and 'after the resurrection', the former period characterized by humiliation and suffering, the latter by power and glory. The phase of humiliation clearly had its culmination in Jesus' death and burial; the phase of glory just as clearly had its historical origin in His resurrection from the dead, and constituted for Jesus an advance over His previous position: the Son of God in evident weakness became, by virtue of His resurrection, the Son of God in manifest power. 'By his resurrection and ascension the Son of God incarnate entered upon a new phase of sovereignty and was endowed with new power correspondent with and unto the exercise of the mediatorial lordship which he executes as head over all things to his body, the church.'[37]

*3.* It is significant that in connection with the events described in verse 4 Paul applies to Jesus the title 'Lord': it is 'Jesus Christ our Lord' who has been thus exalted. And, as Murray reminds us, it is no thoughtless formula that Paul uses here; rather, 'each name has its own peculiar associations and significance . . . "Lord" indicates the lordship to which he is exalted at the right hand of the Father in virtue of which he exercises all authority in heaven and in earth.'[38] The teaching of this passage thus corresponds closely to what was found in Philippians 2:9—11 and Acts 2:36. The significance of this correspondence was not lost on George Ladd: 'Paul concludes the passage by calling Jesus "our Lord", for His becoming the Son of God in power is precisely parallel to the bestowal of lordship in Philippians 2:9.'[39]

## The authority belonging to Jesus as Lord

As noted in the previous chapter, the root idea of lordship is that of authority — legal authority, authority rightfully exercised. While this idea has surfaced in our discussion of the three passages above (especially in Philippians 2:9–11, and to a lesser degree in Acts 2:36), it still remains for us to examine several New Testament passages which treat more specifically of the nature of that authority which belongs to Jesus by virtue of His position as Lord. This will lay the foundation for a later treatment of the Christian's relationship to Jesus and to His authority.

*Matthew 28:18.* One of the clearest claims to authority uttered by Jesus is found at the end of Matthew's Gospel: 'All authority has been given to Me in heaven and on earth' (Matt. 28:18). Several observations are pertinent to our present discussion.

1. The authority that Jesus here speaks of is an authority which was given or granted to Him. Such is the meaning of *didōmi* as used in this context.[40] The aorist passive verb indicates the passivity of Jesus in being granted this authority (it was conferred upon Him by another) as well as the definiteness of the point in time when He received it (implying perhaps that there was a time — in His incarnate existence — when He did not possess it). All this is further emphasized by the occurrence of the verb and the pronoun at the beginning of the sentence, giving a majestic and authoritative ring to the whole pronouncement: '*It has been given to*

*Me* all authority in heaven and on earth.'

2. This pronouncement is made by Jesus *after* His resurrection. While Jesus certainly claimed authority for Himself on other occasions, it is significant that nothing approaching the comprehensiveness of this claim is to be found prior to the resurrection.[41] It is thus reasonable to infer, and accords well with the passages already examined, that the authority claimed by Jesus in this verse was bestowed on Him when He was raised from the dead. This adds support to the contention that a fundamental change in Jesus' status took place at His resurrection and exaltation: He was transferred from the position of one who willingly placed Himself under the authority of men to a position of supreme authority over men and over the universe.

3. Jesus claims for Himself a universal authority. It encompasses no less than 'heaven and earth', a phrase which may indeed speak of heaven as 'standing independently beside the earth' (as Arndt-Gingrich-Danker suggest) but which also seems to imply 'the totality of creation'.[42] In any case it must certainly be a most comprehensive authority which is in view; there is no part of creation that does not come under its sway. The supremacy of this authority is heightened by the phrase 'all authority' (*pasa exousia*), which may be understood as 'absolute authority',[43] indicating that there is (under God) no authority superior to that possessed by Jesus. This affirmation by Jesus is nothing less than a claim to absolute lordship: 'He who has *exousia* is *kyrios*', writes W. Foerster,[44] who elsewhere concurs that the *exousia* claimed by Jesus in

Matthew 28:18 refers to His exaltation as Lord and Christ, parallel to Acts 2:36.[45]

It may be objected that the authority claimed by Jesus in Matthew 28:18 could not be that authority attaching to His mediatorial lordship because, as we have seen, that mediatorial authority is commonly represented in the New Testament as having been bestowed at the time of Jesus' ascension to the right hand of God (Acts 2:33–36; cf. Eph. 1:20–23). To this it may be replied that the resurrection is the first stage of and implies the whole of the exaltation. As A. B. Bruce has written, the ascension is 'conceived as involved in the resurrection'.[46] A fine note on the theology of Matthew 28:18, including the relationship between the resurrection and ascension, may be found in J. P. Lange's commentary on Matthew in the series bearing his name. Lange writes, 'According to the true conception, the ascension is essentially implied in the resurrection. Both events are combined in the one fact of Christ's exaltation. The resurrection is the root and the beginning of the ascension; the ascension is the blossom and crown of the resurrection . . . But this [resurrection] life, as regards its essence, is the heavenly life; and, as regards its character, the entrance into that estate was accordingly the beginning of the ascension. The resurrection marks the entrance into the heavenly *state*; the ascension, into the heavenly *sphere*.'[47]

Thus, while the exaltation is generally regarded as occurring when Jesus ascends to the right hand of the Father, it is not improper for Jesus to speak of His being granted mediatorial authority even before the ascension; for His investiture with authority began immediately upon His entrance into the glorified state, that is, at the resurrection.

4.  It is on the basis of the authority claimed by Jesus that He issues the command found in  verses 19—20. The particle *oun* ('therefore') occurs near the beginning of verse 19,[48] linking it with verse 18, indicating thus both the authority by which Jesus speaks and the authority by which His disciples are to act. He speaks as one who has been given all authority in heaven and earth, and thus He commands His church; His disciples are to go, preach, baptize and teach in that same authority, as those who have been duly authorized by Him. Jesus is seen here in the actual exercise of that authority which is His as exalted Lord; it is to be understood as involving not only His right to rule the universe in a cosmic sense, but also the right to direct His church as He sees fit.[49]

*Ephesians 1:20—23.*   A passage which further defines the nature of Jesus' authority as mediatorial Lord is Ephesians 1:20—23. While the sentence in which this passage is found begins much earlier than verse 20 (it starts in verse 15, according to the twenty-fifth edition of the Nestle-Aland Greek Testament), it is in this verse that Paul begins to expound the doctrine of Jesus' exaltation in a way that is germane to our present discussion. This entire passage (vv. 15—23) is a prayer expressing Paul's desire for the spiritual enlightenment of the Christians to whom he is writing, that they might understand, among other things, the greatness of God's power which is at work in believers (v. 19) — a power comparable to that which God exercised in raising

Christ from the dead and exalting Him to His right hand (v. 20). It is in the second half of this comparison, occupying verses 20—23, that Paul treats of the exaltation of Christ; a perusal of the passage yields the following observations.

*1.* It may once again be seen that the exaltation of Jesus was accomplished in conjunction with His resurrection (v. 20). It is evident that Paul has in view in verses 20—22 a connected series of events ('raised Him . . . seated Him . . . put all things in subjection . . .') which when taken together constitute the exaltation of Christ and demonstrate the greatness of God's power. The necessary first element in this process is the raising of Jesus from the dead, which, as we have already seen, marked His entrance into the exalted state. Apart from the resurrection, there could be no exaltation; in the resurrection, the exaltation was begun.

*2.* The exaltation of Jesus involved His installation in a position of supreme authority. After raising Him from the dead, God 'seated Him at His right hand' (v. 20), a phrase which derives from Psalm 110:1 and which is 'a figurative expression for the place of highest honour and authority'.[50] For Jesus to be seated at the right hand of God means nothing less than 'participation in dominion',[51] a sharing in the throne and lordship of the Father.

Christ's position at the right hand of God is perhaps the most commonly used expression of His exaltation and lordship to be found in the New Testament. It is a favourite of the apostolic church, being found in a wide range of writers and speakers: Peter (Acts 2:33—35; 5:31; 1 Peter 3:22), Stephen (Acts 7:55—56), Paul

(Rom. 8:34; Eph. 1:20; Col. 3:1) and the writer of Hebrews (Heb. 1:3, 13; 8:1; 10:12; 12:2). The expression is also found on the lips of Jesus Himself in all the synoptic Gospels on two occasions: in His question concerning the Davidic sonship of Messiah (Matt. 22: 44; Mark 12:36; Luke 20:42), and in His confession before the Sanhedrin (Matt. 26:64; Mark 14:62; Luke 22:69). The pervasive use in the New Testament of this phrase from Psalm 110 is not without significance for our present study; as Cullmann has observed, 'Nothing indicates better than the very frequent citation of this very psalm how vital was the present lordship of Christ in early Christian thought. It is quoted not just in a few isolated places, but throughout the whole New Testament. Almost no other Old Testament passage is cited so often.'[52] The use of this single phrase (occurring some twenty times in the New Testament) constitutes a weighty demonstration that the early church put great emphasis on the exaltation and lordship of Jesus.

3. The lordship which Jesus exercises involves His supremacy (as mediatorial Lord, under God the Father) over all other authority in the universe. This is indicated by three elements in verses 21–22a. (i) His position is said to be 'high above [*hyperanō,* referring to rank, power[53]] all rule and authority and power and dominion' (v. 21a). The four categories mentioned here (respectively: *archē, exousia, dynamis, kyriotē*) are commonly understood to represent 'familiar distinctions of spiritual forces',[54] that is, classes of supernatural spirit-beings, whether angelic or demonic.[55] While some interpreters apparently do not regard Paul as viewing these spirit-forces as 'objective realities',[56]

Paul's own words elsewhere would seem to indicate otherwise. At the end of Ephesians he writes that 'our struggle is not against flesh and blood, but against the rulers, against the powers, against the world forces of this darkness, against the spiritual forces of wickedness in the heavenly places' (Eph. 6:12). The first two terms here, 'rulers' and 'powers', are the same as the first two in 1:21. These two categories are also mentioned in Ephesians 3:10, where Paul states that it is part of the eternal purpose of God to make known through the church His manifold wisdom 'to the *rulers* and the *authorities* in the heavenly places'. In these instances Paul certainly seems to regard the spirit-forces as possessing objective reality. In any case, it is true that 'the apostle's purpose in mentioning them . . . is to emphasize the exaltation of Christ above them all'.[57]

The importance which the early church attached to Christ's lordship over the spirit-forces has been noted by Cullmann,[58] and is indicated in the New Testament by the frequency with which the concept is mentioned. Christ is not only the Creator of these spirit-forces (Col. 1:16), but through His triumph on the cross He has disarmed and displayed those which were hostile to Him (Col. 2:15), so that He is now 'the head over all rule and authority' (Col. 2:10). His exaltation to the right hand of God means that 'angels and authorities and powers' have been subjected to Him (1 Peter 3:22). Eventually, 'when He has abolished all rule and all authority and power,' Christ will 'deliver up the kingdom' to the Father (1 Cor. 15:24). When to these references there are added the three already noted in Ephesians, it becomes clear that this theme carried considerable significance for the New Testament writers.

(ii) Jesus is also said to have been exalted far above 'every name that is named, not only in this age, but also in the one to come' (Eph. 1:21b). This very comprehensive statement means that there is no power or authority that will surpass that of Christ, either before the consummation or after. His name is above all others (cf. Phil. 2:9—11). 'Above all that anywhere is, anywhere can be — above all grades of dignity, real or imagined, good or evil, present or to come — the mighty power of God has exalted and enthroned the Christ.'[59]

(iii) God, in exalting Christ, is said to have 'put all things in subjection under His feet' (Eph. 1:22a). This is also a broad and comprehensive statement of the authority possessed by Christ as exalted Lord, indicating (in the words of Westcott) that 'He is invested with universal sovereignty'.[60] A more comprehensive expression than this would be difficult to imagine: 'all things' (*panta*) have been 'put in subjection' (*hypetaxen*, aorist) under (the feet of) Christ. These words attribute to Christ an authority that is universal in scope and absolute in degree.

4. The authority of the exalted Christ includes His lordship over the church (vv. 22b—23). Lordship is here defined in terms of headship, not a synonymous but a related concept, which in this context denotes 'superior rank'.[61] Paul's mode of expression here is not as clear as it is in Ephesians 4:15 and 5:23 ('Christ is the head of the church'), which has given rise to diverse interpretations of 1:22b. Some, such as F. F. Bruce, understand the phrase 'head over all things' to mean 'supreme head', and relate it directly to Christ's

position as 'supreme head of the church'.[62] Others, for example, William Hendriksen, understand the 'all things' of verse 22b to be as comprehensive as the same phrase in 22a, and thus believe that 'Christ is not actually said to be the head of the church, but rather "head over everything to the church"'. Christ is given to the church as the One who is Head over all things and *in its interests* he exercises his infinite power in causing the entire universe with all that is in it to co-operate, whether willingly or unwillingly'.[63] On the basis of the former interpretation, Christ is explicitly said to be the Head of the church; on the basis of the latter, He is said to be Head over all things, which would then include the church. At any rate, Paul in verse 23 identifies the church as Christ's body, a connection which virtually demands that the headship mentioned in verse 22 be understood to include the church, regardless of whether a larger sphere of authority is also in view. Thus the authority belonging to the exalted Lord Jesus involves in a special sense His lordship or headship over the church as well as His lordship over the universe.

*Romans 14:9.* The final passage we will consider in the present connection is Romans 14:9. In the course of Paul's argument concerning Christian liberty in the fourteenth chapter of Romans, he makes this assertion: 'For to this end Christ died and lived again, that He might be Lord both of the dead and of the living.' Again, let us make some observations on the text.

1. The death and resurrection of Jesus are said to be connected with regard to their purpose; that is, it was the divine intention that by means of these two

events Jesus might become Lord of the dead and the living. The purpose clause with which the sentence begins (*eis touto*[64]) links together in a single purpose the two aspects of Jesus' redemptive work, His death and resurrection (*apethanen kai ezēsen*, 'died and lived', should be so understood[65]). The assertion is that He died and rose again in order that this purpose might be fulfilled.

2. It was specifically in order to attain lordship over the dead and the living[66] that Jesus died and lived again. It is not the noun *kyrios* that is used here to express lordship, but the verb *kyrieuō*, meaning 'to be lord' or 'master' or 'to rule'.[67] Its subjunctive mood again indicates the purpose that was in view in Jesus' death and resurrection, and its position at the end of the sentence gives added emphasis to the thought. Paul is affirming that it was in order to achieve this concrete purpose, the gaining of lordship or rulership over those persons who are in view, that Jesus suffered the anguish of the cross and was raised in glory by the power of the Father. This is a clear statement of broad scope indicating the divine purpose in the saving work of Christ; that purpose was no less than the establishment of His lordship over those for whom He died and lived again.

3. The 'dead and the living' over whom the lordship of Christ is established must in this context be restricted to those who belong to Christ, that is, Christian believers. While there is not universal agreement on this point,[68] the preceding verses certainly seem to demand this restriction. In this passage Paul is warning against a censorious attitude among Christians on matters of conduct where liberty is permitted. He

appeals to the exclusiveness of the master-slave relationship between Christ and the believer in verse 4a (applying the term *kyrios* to Christ) as grounds for his exhortation that believers are not to judge one another. He refers each man's observance or non-observance as unto the Lord (Paul's usual title for Jesus, v. 6). The whole of every Christian's life, and even his death, is not for himself but for the Lord (vv. 7—8), this fact being grounded not in the subjective 'faith which is consciously exercised by the believer' but in the objective 'relation which Christ sustains to him, namely, that of possession'.[69]

While Paul makes these assertions with respect to *every* believer (he envisages no exceptions: *'Not one of us* lives for himself,' v. 7), it is likewise the case that they are made with exclusive reference to believers. It is specifically the living and dying of believers that is in view in verses 7—8; and it is over believers both dead and living (v. 9b; Paul reverses the order to conform to the dying and living — crucifixion and resurrection — of Christ) that Christ establishes His lordship by means of His redemptive work. While it is certainly true that there is a broader and more universal aspect of the lordship of Christ, it must be maintained that such is not in view in this passage. Thus we agree with Murray's conclusion that 'because of the context it would not be feasible to understand this text as having all-inclusive reference'.[70] We may with good warrant understand Paul as saying that it was for the express purpose of establishing His lordship over believers that Christ died and rose again.

4. We must regard the purpose in view in Christ's death and resurrection as finding actual (not potential)

fulfilment in all believers. Jesus is in fact Lord over all Christians by virtue of His possession of them. Paul's language demands this conclusion; in its support appeal may be made to much of the same evidence noted above: (i) In the analogy of verse 4a he speaks of Christ as the Master or Lord (*kyrios*) and the believer as a servant. (ii) In verses 7—8a, Paul says that 'not one of us' lives or dies unto or for himself, but for the Lord (Jesus). (iii) In 8b he says that 'we are the Lord's', indicating the objective relationship of possession and thus the legitimate right of control. Nowhere in these verses does Paul intimate that he is speaking of a special group of Christians who have acknowledged the lordship of Christ as distinct from those who have not; he simply assumes that for every believer Jesus is Lord, both by right and by confession.

5. Finally, an observation made with respect to several other passages may be repeated here: the lordship over believers ascribed to Jesus in Romans 14:9 is a position that was attained by Him through His death and resurrection, and thus differs from that sovereignty which He possesses and exercises by inherent right as God the Son. It follows that it is not merely His deity which is in view in the ascription to Him of lordship over believers, for He was God apart from His death and resurrection, whereas the lordship attributed to Him here required His redeeming work in order for its accomplishment to be realized. Paul says that it was '*to this end*' that 'Christ died and lived again, that He might be Lord both of the dead and of the living'. As Murray has written, 'The lordship of Christ here dealt with did not belong to Christ by native right as the Son

of God; it had to be secured. It is the lordship of redemptive relationship and such did not inhere in the sovereignty that belongs to him in virtue of his creatorhood. It is achieved by mediatorial accomplishment and is the reward of his humiliation.'[71] The lordship of Jesus over believers belongs to Him by right of His peculiar possession of them, which was secured by His redemptive work in their behalf.[72]

## Summary

We have found, then, in examining these six passages (and others related to them), that (i) the resurrection of Jesus marked the beginning of a new phase of His career, that of exaltation; (ii) Jesus' exaltation consisted in His being seated at the right hand of God and His being granted the title 'Lord'; (iii) the authority attaching to this position of lordship is supreme and absolute, and encompasses both the universe in general and the church in particular; (iv) the doctrine of Jesus' lordship occupied a prominent place in the faith of the early church and is found throughout the New Testament. Building on these conclusions, we turn now to a consideration of the proclamation and confession of Jesus' lordship.

# 3
# Jesus is Lord: the basic New Testament confession

The prominence given to the doctrine of the mediatorial lordship of Jesus in the early church's faith (as observed in the previous chapter) naturally leads us to ask, 'Did the lordship of Jesus occupy a similarly prominent place in the proclamation of the church?' Was it a fundamental element in the first preaching of the gospel (or to use the technical term, the first *kērygma*)? And if it was, for what purpose? Did the early preachers of the gospel seek to elicit some particular response to the fact of Jesus' lordship? This chapter will address these questions as we examine in turn the proclamation of the early church and the confession which that proclamation called forth.

## The proclaiming of Jesus as Lord

We have already observed that the first apostolic proclamation of the gospel was climaxed by the announcement that God had made Jesus to be Lord (Acts 2:33—36). This emphasis on the exaltation and lordship of Jesus in Peter's Pentecost sermon was no accident or fluke, but was characteristic of the preaching of the early church. Virtually every evangelistic address found in Acts includes mention of the exaltation and lordship of Jesus. Those which do not refer specifically to Jesus' lordship do speak of His resurrection, which, as we noted earlier, is the first stage of His exaltation and which, even before the ascension, involved the conferment of mediatorial authority (Matt. 28:18).

Besides Acts 2:33—36, we may note the following passages in Acts. In Peter's evangelistic address at the temple recorded in chapter 3, Jesus is referred to as 'the Christ appointed for you, whom heaven must receive until the period of restoration of all things' (Acts 3:20—21), an obvious allusion to the ascension and present exalted state of Jesus.

When, in Acts 5, Peter replies to the Sanhedrin's demand that the apostles stop preaching in Jesus' name, he tells them that Jesus 'is the one whom God exalted to His right hand as a Prince [*archēgos*, "leader, ruler, prince"[1] ] and a Saviour', a reference to Jesus' position of authority as exalted Lord.

Later, when Stephen is on trial before the same group, he speaks (at the risk of his life) of Jesus' exaltation: 'Behold, I see the heavens opened up and the Son of Man standing at the right hand of God' (Acts 7:56) — which utterance led immediately to his being stoned by his Jewish hearers.

When Peter preaches to the household of Cornelius, he declares that Jesus is 'Lord of all' (Acts 10:36), and that in His exalted state He 'has been appointed by God as Judge of the living and the dead' (Acts 10:42).

When those who are scattered by 'the persecution

that arose in connection with Stephen' reach Syrian Antioch, they begin 'speaking to the Greeks also, preaching the *Lord* Jesus' (Acts 11:20, emphasis mine).

The first of Paul's evangelistic addresses to be recorded in Acts is found in chapter 13. Preaching in Pisidian Antioch to a predominantly Jewish audience, Paul gives heavy emphasis to the resurrection of Jesus (Acts 13:30—37), a passage which may contain an oblique reference to the exaltation: in verse 33 he offers Old Testament support for the resurrection of Christ by quoting Psalm 2:7, a psalm which speaks above all else of Messiah's installation as Jehovah's appointed King (Ps. 2:6—9). If the context of Psalm 2:7 is thus taken into account, as well as the place of the resurrection in the exaltation of Jesus, then a reference by Paul to the exaltation would seem to be implied.

Later, in Acts 16, when Paul is asked by the jailer at Philippi concerning the way of salvation, he replies, 'Believe in the *Lord* Jesus, and you shall be saved' (Acts 16:31, emphasis mine).

When some Christians in Thessalonica are dragged before the city authorities by a Jewish-organized mob, they are accused of acting 'contrary to the decrees of Caesar, saying that there is another king, Jesus' (Acts 17:7). It is significant that here the Christian message is characterized by its enemies (though admittedly without full understanding) as asserting that Jesus is king (*basileus*), a title which, in the words of Cullmann, is 'a variant of the *Kyrios* title'.[2]

Paul's speech at Athens may also contain an indirect reference to the exaltation of Jesus. In Acts 17:31 Paul offers the resurrection of Jesus as proof of his assertion that God has appointed Jesus as that Man through whom God will judge the world — the exercise of judgement certainly being the prerogative only of one who possesses supreme authority.

The rest of the major addresses in Acts are not evangelistic in nature (Paul's farewell to the Ephesian elders, 20:17—35; his defence of himself before various bodies, 22:1—21; 24:10—21; 26:1—23), but it may be noted that the emphasis on Jesus' resurrection continues (Acts 25:19; 26:8). Indeed, Paul's conversion experience, which he recounts in his speeches in Acts 22 and 26, is nothing less than a vision of the risen, glorified and exalted Lord Jesus.

This brief survey of Acts suggests that it can at least be said that there is no element of apostolic preaching more prominent than the resurrection, exaltation and lordship of Jesus. Other research on the content of the apostolic *kērygma* confirms this impression. For example, Robert H. Mounce, in a formulation of the early *kērygma* that is somewhat more biblical and more accurate than that of C. H. Dodd,[3] suggests that the *kērygma* consisted of three elements: 'a historical proclamation, a theological evaluation, and an ethical summons'.[4] These are respectively, (i) a proclamation of the death, resurrection and exaltation of Jesus, seen as the fulfilment of prophecy and involving man's responsibility; (ii) the resultant evaluation of Jesus as both Lord and Christ; (iii) a summons to repent and receive forgiveness of sins.[5]

Mounce's formulation is based primarily on the examples of apostolic preaching found in Acts, but he shows that it is also in harmony with those kerygmatic passages in the Pauline Epistles which are possibly pre-Pauline in origin and which thus indicate the nature of the message handed down to Paul (1 Cor. 15:3–5; Rom. 10:9; 1:3–4; 4:24–25; 8:34).[6]

It may be noted that Mounce, in his outline of the characteristic elements of the *kērygma,* refers in his first point to the proclamation of the resurrection and exaltation of Jesus (which is so obvious in Acts as to need no demonstration here) leading on to the announcement of Jesus' lordship and messiahship, in support of which Mounce adduces Acts 2:34, 36; 3:19–20 and 10:36, passages from the major evangelistic addresses of Peter. Mounce concludes, 'No matter how far we move back into the dawn of apostolic preaching, there we find as its very heart and core the proclamation that Jesus of Nazareth is "both Lord and Christ".'[7] In a similar vein is the comment by F. F. Bruce, offered in another connection but relevant here: 'From the earliest days of the apostolic preaching the resurrection and enthronement of Christ were proclaimed side by side as integral to the good news.'[8] It would seem that a careful perusal of the book of Acts could lead to no other conclusion.

We are not entirely dependent, however, on the preaching found in Acts for a proper conception of the apostolic message. Paul himself, in 2 Corinthians 4:5, provides a broad characterization of the preached message: 'For we do not preach ourselves but Christ Jesus as Lord, and ourselves as your bond-servants for Jesus' sake.' This comprehensive statement must be taken as co-ordinate with and complementary to such passages as 1 Corinthians 2:2 (where Paul's purpose requires an emphasis on Jesus as the crucified One). It may be observed with regard to 2 Corinthians 4:5 that (i) Paul here characterizes the preaching of a broader company than just his own person, as indicated by his use of the first person plural verb ('we preach'). (ii) Paul uses the Greek word *kērussō*, whose basic meaning is 'to announce' as a herald,[9] signifying the authoritative and reliable transmission of a message which one has received and is not at liberty to alter. (iii) The content of the message is *Iēsoun Christon kyrion*, 'Jesus Christ as Lord',[10] that is, Jesus Christ as the exalted Saviour and Sovereign of the universe. 'In his [Paul's] gospel the glory is of Christ, and accordingly the burden of its proclamation is Christ Jesus *as Lord (Kyrios),* for the Lordship of Christ is central and altogether indispensable to the evangelical message.'[11] In this verse we have it from Paul himself that 'the heart of the apostolic kerygma is the proclamation of the Lordship of Jesus'.[12] This emphasis stands not in opposition to the preaching of Christ crucified (1 Cor. 2:2), but as complementary to it: it is Jesus in His identity as the crucified One who has now been exalted as Lord, and He is so proclaimed by the apostolic message.

Another passage that is germane to our discussion is Romans 10:8—10, where Paul brings together the two elements which form the subject of this chapter, the proclamation and the confession of Jesus' lordship. We will give attention now to the first of these, and following that, to the content and meaning of the confession which the apostolic preaching intended to elicit.

In Romans 10:6—8 Paul is drawing support for the doctrine of justification by faith from Deuteronomy 30:12—14. In verse 8 he identifies the 'word' of Deuteronomy 30:14 with the 'word of faith which we are preaching', namely, 'that if you confess with your mouth Jesus as Lord, and believe in your heart that God raised Him from the dead, you shall be saved' (v. 9). These verses reveal two important facts about the apostolic *kērygma*. In the first place, there was essentially one common message. Paul again uses the first person plural of *kērussō* ('we preach', v. 8), indicating that it is not merely his own personal message that he is describing but one that was commonly accepted and proclaimed by a broader community. Verse 9 is thus 'a concise summary of the "word of faith" that was everywhere proclaimed by the apostles and the missionary church. Since Paul assumes his readers' knowledge of this "word of faith", we may infer that it is both common to all the apostles and pre-Pauline in origin.'[13]

In the second place, this passage demonstrates that the lordship of Jesus was integral to the message. Verse 9 is a description not only of the confession elicited but of the message proclaimed. The confession that 'Jesus is Lord' is 'not only related to the proclamation but is actually a part of the kerygma'.[14] It is only natural that the confession which the gospel seeks should itself be found as a vital element in the church's preaching. 'The essentials of the gospel which the church proclaimed were closely related to the *homologia* [confession] to which the Christian community adhered'[15] and which it sought from its converts.

## The confession of Jesus as Lord

The confession 'Jesus is Lord' is the single most pre-dominant Christian confession in the New Testament. Not only does it occur in several passages which empha-size its singular character as *the* Christian confession (e.g., Phil. 2:9–11; Rom. 10:9; 1 Cor. 12:3; 8:5–6; cf. Eph. 4:5), but it also occurs numerous times in a variant form in the phrase 'our Lord', a designation of Jesus which was so widely used that it became the dis-tinctive and universally recognized Christian confession, known and acknowledged by all believers.[16]

While it is perhaps going too far to say with Mounce that 'Jesus is Lord' was the 'earliest single-clause Christological confession of primitive Christianity',[17] it is correct to say that it soon became the prevailing form of Christian confession. By the time of Paul it was predominant. As Neufeld observes, 'The evidence clearly indicates that the basic *homologia* in the Pauline Epistles is the simple formula *kyrios Iēsous*';[18] and he goes on to point out, 'The *homologia* itself was in all likelihood received by Paul from the primitive church.'[19] In other words, this confession probably did not originate with Paul; it was received by him as a confession commonly known and used in the church, and his use of it therefore reflects an early and broad theological tradition.

The word *homologeō*, translated 'confess' in Romans 10:9, literally means 'to say the same thing' or 'to agree in statement';[20] and by the time of the New Testament era it could bear the meaning 'to make solemn state-

ments of faith' or 'to confess something in faith'.[21]
It is used in this sense in Romans 10:9—10 and several
other places in the New Testament (John 9:22; 1 John
4:2, 15; etc.). Neufeld, following his study of the word,
concludes that in such instances it has the significance
of personal acceptance and acknowledgement of a truth
adhered to by the entire community of believers. 'The
*homologia* represented the agreement or consensus in
which the Christian community was united, that core of
essential conviction and belief to which Christians sub-
scribed and openly testified.'[22] And one truth in which
the Christian community was united was the lordship of
Jesus Christ.

*The meaning of the confession.* The present writer
suggests that the confession 'Jesus is Lord' (Rom. 10:9,
etc.) is quite broad in scope and involves four related
but distinguishable elements.

   *1.* It involves the acknowledgement of Jesus' position as exalted Lord. This fundamental theme of apostolic preaching naturally finds a prominent place in the
Christian confession. And it should be noted, as Murray
states, 'how far-reaching are the implications' of this
confession. It explicitly affirms the exaltation of Jesus,
and implies all that preceded the exaltation; the whole
redemptive work of Christ is in view in this single statement. 'The confession "Jesus as Lord" or "Jesus is
Lord" refers to the lordship which Jesus exercises in
virtue of his exaltation . . . This lordship presupposes
the incarnation, death, and resurrection of Christ and
consists in his investiture with universal dominion.'[23]

   The hearer of the gospel message is called upon to

affirm 'an article of faith, namely, that by virtue of his death and resurrection, Jesus has been exalted to a place of sovereignty over all men'.[24] Again it may be said that the lordship of Jesus does not stand in opposition to His atoning work, but is the culmination and fulfilment of it, as well as His personal vindication. Thus all the basic facts of the gospel story are implicit in the single brief confession, 'Jesus is Lord'.[25]

*2.* This confession involves the acknowledgement of the rightful authority of Jesus Christ over the believer. This is implied by the basic meaning of the title 'Lord' (see Chapter 1), by the position of Jesus as the exalted Sovereign, and by His legal possession of the believer (1 Cor. 6:19—20); and it is indicated in the New Testament by the nearly universal Christian designation of Jesus as 'our Lord'. The broad purpose of God is to bring all things under the authority of Christ (Ps. 2; 1 Cor. 15:25—28; Phil. 2:9—11); the Christian is one who willingly enters the sphere of that acknowledged authority when he confesses Jesus as Lord. This confession, says Ladd, 'reflects the personal experience of the confessor. He confesses Jesus as Lord because he has received Jesus Christ as *his* Lord (Col. 2:6). He has entered into a new relationship in which he acknowledges the absolute sovereignty and mastery of the exalted Jesus over his life'.[26]

*3.* This confession involves the acknowledgement of the deity of Jesus Christ. Cranfield argues persuasively that the Septuagint usage of *kyrios* as God's name should play an important part in understanding the designation of Jesus as *kyrios*. 'The use of *kyrios* more than six thousand times in the LXX to represent the Tetragrammaton must surely be regarded as of decisive importance here.' After summarizing several substantial lines of reasoning, he concludes that 'the confession that Jesus is Lord meant the acknowledgement that Jesus shares the name and the nature, the holiness, the authority, power, majesty and eternity of the one and only true God'.[27]

4. This confession involves personal trust in Jesus Christ. It hardly needs to be said that the utterance of this confession must be more than just an empty ritual or the expression of an arid intellectualism; Paul regards it as reflecting the sincere conviction, humble trust and submissive attitude of the believer's mind and heart. The 'confessing' of Romans 10:9—10 assumes the prior act of 'believing' mentioned in these same verses; and together they are such confessing and believing as result in 'righteousness' and 'salvation' (v. 10). Nor is there any disjunction between the two. The lordship of Jesus (which is confessed, v. 9a) is intimately connected with His resurrection (which is believed, v. 9b), as we have already seen. 'The content of the confession and the content of the belief are differently formulated, but in Paul's thought they amount to the same thing. He does not mean to imply that the mouth is to confess anything other than that which the heart believes.'[28]

All of which is to say that this confession is a confession *of faith*, a faith by which one enters into a personal relationship with Jesus Christ the Lord. Since confession implies believing, and since 'Lord' implies the whole of Jesus' work, then to confess Him as Lord is to trust Him and receive Him in the fulness of who

He is and what He has done. It means to believe in Him as the Son of God, the crucified Saviour and exalted Lord. It means to appropriate to oneself the benefits of all His redeeming work, past, present and future. It means to take upon oneself the responsibilities which are entailed in personal submission to the Sovereign of the universe.

It has been stated above that the confession of Jesus as Lord involves the acknowledgement of the rightful authority of Jesus Christ over the confessor. This authority or lordship of Jesus over the individual believer may be regarded as grounded in two facts: creation and redemption. God holds a rightful claim upon every individual by virtue of His creation of the world and all that is in it. The cattle on a thousand hills are His, and every beast of the forest: 'the world is Mine, and all it contains' (Ps. 50:10, 12; see also Ps. 104:24; 24:1; 89:11). Every human being belongs to God by right of creation and owes to his Creator love and service, obedience and submission (Mark 12: 28–34; the great commandment can by legitimate extension be applied to all men). Since the resurrection of Jesus, God exercises His authority over men through Christ the Lord, and for men to confess His lordship is to recognize His legitimate authority as Creator.

The second ground of Jesus' authority over believers is redemption. In biblical usage, to redeem means to purchase; Jesus, by means of His redemptive work on behalf of His people, has purchased them for Himself, with the result that they no longer belong to themselves, but to Him. 'Do you not know,' Paul writes to the Christians at Corinth, '. . . that you are not your own? For you have been bought with a price: therefore glorify God in your body' (1 Cor. 6:19, 20). The basis of the ethical obligation here is the fact of the divine redemption and ownership of believers. The word translated 'bought' is *agorazō*, meaning here 'buy, acquire as property'.[29] It is used in a similar sense with reference to believers in 1 Corinthians 7:23 and Revelation 5:9 (cf. also Acts 20:28, where a different verb is used). Jesus' possession of believers is also affirmed in Romans 14:8, a passage we have already examined: 'Whether we live or die, we are the Lord's.' It is thus on these two grounds, creation and redemption, that the Christian is obligated to acknowledge the rightful authority of God over him, and in confessing Jesus as Lord he indeed does so.

*The centrality of the confession.* Besides Romans 10:9, there are several other New Testament passages in which the confession 'Jesus is Lord' is identified as the characteristic and distinctive Christian confession. We have already examined Philippians 2:9—11, with its affirmation of the universal confession of Jesus' lordship at the consummation. Another passage which demonstrates the centrality of this confession is 1 Corinthians 12:3: 'Therefore I make known to you, that no one speaking by the Spirit of God says, "Jesus is accursed"; and no one can say, "Jesus is Lord", except by the Holy Spirit.' Cursing Jesus is clearly set in opposition to confessing Him as Lord; the contrast is between the Christian acknowledgement of Jesus and the anti-Christian view of Him, the former being defined as confessing His lordship. Neufeld and Cullmann suggest that the context here may be that of state persecution, in which some professing Christians yielded to the pressure to curse Jesus and then claimed the guidance of the Holy Spirit in doing so.[30] Paul of course affirms the opposite: that the Spirit of God leads one not to curse Jesus but rather to acknowledge that 'Jesus is Lord' (*kyrios Iēsous*). The life situation in view here cannot be determined with certainty. It is clear, however, that in this verse 'the importance of this confession in the Pauline churches is vividly set forth'.[31]

Opposition, this time from paganism, is perhaps also in view in 1 Corinthians 8:5—6.[32] In this passage Paul acknowledges that there are indeed many so-called gods and lords (v. 5), but for Christians 'there is but one God, the Father, from whom are all things, and we exist for Him; and one Lord, Jesus Christ, through whom are all things, and we exist through Him' (v. 6). When the question of the essential distinction between Christianity and paganism arose, the Christian faith was distinguished by its confession of one God, the Father, and one Lord, Jesus Christ. Surely such a confession must be expected to define the heart of the Christian faith; and at its heart is found the acknowledgement of the lordship of Jesus.

There are other New Testament passages which give indication of being creed-like formulas or confessions. Ephesians 4:4—6 includes the three Persons of the triune God: there is 'one Spirit . . . one Lord . . . one God and Father'. 'Lord' here must refer to Christ. Some writers regard Romans 1:3—4 as a pre-Pauline confessional or kerygmatic formula.[33] It designates the exalted Jesus as 'Lord' and as the 'Son of God in power'. Mounce believes that Romans 4:24—25 may also fall into this category.[34] This passage describes Christians as 'those who believe in Him who raised Jesus our Lord from the dead, He who was delivered up because of our transgressions, and was raised because of our justification'. Both the death and resurrection of Jesus are mentioned, and He is again designated 'Lord'. Such passages may or may not be confessional in nature; some would appear to be so. In any case, they lend corroborating support to the view that the lordship of Jesus was central to early Christianity. And the evidence taken as a whole leaves little doubt about the fact.

*The corporate nature of the confession.* There is a phenomenon in the New Testament which is often overlooked (it seems) but which convincingly demonstrates that the confession 'Jesus is Lord' was not only central to the New Testament faith, but also that it was universally recognized and used among the churches and that it involved personal acknowledgement of the authority of Jesus Christ over believers. This phenomenon is the pervasive use in the New Testament of the simple phrase 'our Lord' in reference to Jesus. This phrase is typically used at the beginning of an Epistle (e.g. Rom. 1:4) or at the conclusion (Rom. 16: 20), but may be found anywhere in between (Rom. 4: 24; 5:1, 11, 21; 6:23; 7:25; 8:39; 15:6, 30; 16:18). The phrase is used in various combinations by Paul (according to Ladd, 'our Lord Jesus Christ', twenty-eight times; 'our Lord Jesus', nine times; 'Jesus Christ our Lord', three times[35]), by the writer of Hebrews

(7:14; 13:20), by James (2:1), by Peter (1 Peter 1:3; 2 Peter 1:2, 8, 11, 14, 16; 3:18), and by Jude (Jude 4, 17, 21, 25). It is also found in Acts (15:26; 20:21). A variant form of the phrase, with the singular pronoun ('my Lord') is found in Philippians 3:8, and in Thomas' confession in John 20:28 ('My Lord and my God'), which Cullmann regards as the climax of the book.[36] The use of this phrase is thus seen to be widespread, both geographically (including Palestine, Syria, the provinces of Asia Minor, Macedonia, Achaia, Italy and Crete — everywhere that Christianity had spread) and among the various writers of the New Testament (it occurs in every New Testament book from the Gospel of John onwards except for Philemon, the Epistles of John and Revelation). It would be difficult to find in the New Testament a more universally used designation of Jesus than 'our Lord'.

That the common designation 'our Lord' was furthermore used early in the life of the young church is demonstrated by the Aramaic phrase *marana tha*, found in 1 Corinthians 16:22. This phrase means 'Our Lord, come', and because of its occurrence in the Aramaic language it must be regarded as having had its origin in the Palestinian church. Thus it appears that 'our Lord' was used as a designation of Jesus from a very early stage of the church's history.[37]

The implications of this phrase for our current investigation are three.

1. It indicates the personal relationship that exists between Jesus Christ and all Christian believers. When, instead of the simple article with 'Lord' to designate Jesus ('the Lord Jesus Christ', etc.), 'there is joined

with the title *kyrios* a personal pronoun in the genitive [*hēmōn*, 'our', etc.], there is expressed . . . the sense of His ownership of those who acknowledge Him and of their consciousness of being His property, the sense of personal commitment and allegiance, of trust and confidence.'[38] It is significant that in the New Testament Christians are never urged to make an initial acknowledgement of Jesus' lordship, nor is any distinction drawn between those who have done so and those who have not; rather, as the phrase 'our Lord' demonstrates, it is simply assumed (as a fact lying at the basis of the Christian faith) that every believer already stands in relation to Jesus as a subject to his Lord. It is naturally expected that every Christian is in sympathy with the expression 'our Lord'.

*2.* In the second place, particular instances of the use of this phrase indicate that there was no disjunction between the Christian's relationship to Jesus as Lord and his relationship to Jesus as Saviour. 2 Peter 1:11 and 3:18 speak of 'our Lord and Saviour Jesus Christ' (in 2:20 the article rather than the pronoun occurs with this designation of Jesus; cf. also 3:2). Peter apparently regards all Christians as sustaining this dual relationship to Jesus, and expects nothing less than instant recognition of this designation and wholehearted assent to its content.

*3.* The third implication of this phrase is that it expresses that by which the Christian community is identified and united. To be a Christian meant to be counted among those who confessed Jesus as 'our Lord'. And not only did this confession identify the church; it also united it. The confessor became a part of that great company of Christian believers throughout the Roman Empire which maintained this common allegiance. One's relationship to Jesus as Lord 'is not alone personal and individualistic; it is a relationship enjoyed by the church as a whole . . . In confessing Jesus as Lord, the confessor joins a fellowship of those who have acknowledged his Lordship.'[39] This was *the* confession common to all Christians. This is what identified them and bound them together; all could say, 'Jesus is [our] Lord.' The New Testament writers could send their Epistles across the empire, refer to Jesus as 'our Lord', and do so in the confidence that their readers would be in absolute sympathy with that expression. It pervades the New Testament as the identifying and unifying confession of the Christian community.

## Objections considered

The interpretation of the confession 'Jesus is Lord' which is set forth here, as well as the estimate of its place in New Testament faith, is disputed by such respected and well-known evangelical scholars as Everett F. Harrison and Charles C. Ryrie. Harrison's objections to this view are found in his *Eternity* article mentioned earlier, while Ryrie's are set forth in chapter 17 of *Balancing the Christian Life*. Both Harrison's article and Ryrie's chapter are entitled 'Must Christ Be Lord to Be Saviour?' and both answer the question in the negative.

It may be pointed out immediately that virtually all the objections urged by these men suffer from a single basic defect: they confuse the Christian's *practice* of the lordship of Christ with the Christian's *acknowledgement in principle* of the lordship of Christ. To require the practical observance of the lordship of Jesus as essential for justification is indeed to add something to biblical 'faith' and to make human works-righteousness the ground of salvation. But that is not the biblical position, nor is it the position advocated here. Rather, the New Testament requires the Christian convert's acknowledgement of the principle that 'Jesus is Lord'; the practical implications of that principle are to be worked out after conversion, within the maturing process of the Christian life.

The major objections to the view herein set forth are three: (i) to require acknowledgement of the lordship of Jesus is to make human works-righteousness the ground of salvation; (ii) there are instances of known believers who were not fully committed to the lordship of Jesus; (iii) to require this acknowledgement leaves no room for the 'carnal Christian'. There are also some miscellaneous objections which will be treated briefly together.

*1.* The most fundamental objection we must consider asserts that requiring acknowledgement of Jesus' lordship makes human works and righteousness the ground of man's salvation. Harrison argues that this view 'involves the introduction of a subtle form of legalism'; it 'brings works in by the side door'.[40] Ryrie regularly speaks of the requirement of this confession as demanding something 'in addition to faith' or 'along with faith' as necessary for salvation.[41]

There are two basic flaws in this objection. They are

(i) as mentioned above, the failure to distinguish between the principle and the practice of the lordship of Jesus, and (ii) an unbiblical view of the nature of saving faith. These two matters are closely related, but we will attempt to deal with them separately.

In the first place, by failing to distinguish between the principle and the practice of the lordship of Jesus, Harrison and Ryrie confuse a change of attitude (the convert's acknowledgement in principle of Jesus' rightful lordship or authority over him) with the results of that change of attitude (the practical observance of Jesus' lordship in the Christian life). The Bible indeed denies that fallen man's works can gain him right standing with God. Man's justification before God is based on the righteousness of Christ alone, imputed to man through faith alone (Rom. 3:21—4:25; Gal. 2:16; 3:6—14; Phil. 3:9). But the Bible also teaches that because of the natural man's enmity against God (Rom. 8:7), there must be a change of mind, a change of attitude, in order for man to enter into a positive relationship with God. This change of attitude the New Testament calls 'repentance' (*metanoia*, 'a change of mind, repentance, turning about, conversion'[42] ), and it involves a reformation of the natural man's thinking—his thinking about God and self, about sin and righteousness, about Christ and salvation. At its most fundamental level, repentance recognizes the right of God the Creator to rule over man the creature; this constitutes an absolute reversal of the natural man's way of thinking (which denies God's right so to rule). Repentance involves no less than a reconstitution of man's world-view, with the result that God rather than man is placed at the centre of the universe. And this, it is suggested, is essentially what is involved in the confession 'Jesus is Lord'. It is instructive to note the conjunction in Acts of the announcement of Jesus' lordship and the preaching of repentance, a connection which would appear to closely relate the two (compare Acts 2:33—36 and v. 38; 3:19 and vv. 20—21; 5:31; 10:36 and 11:18; 17:30 and v. 31).

It was stated previously that the confession of Jesus' lordship means (among other things) 'the acknowledgement of the rightful authority of Jesus Christ over the believer [i.e., the confessor]'. This acknowledgement is no works-righteousness. It does not fall into the category of a human 'work' at all; it is a non-meritorious change of mind and attitude, a simple recognition of plain truth (which furthermore is wrought by God Himself, 1 Cor. 12:3). That is not to say that it has no moral or practical implications. This change of attitude should (and will, in the truly converted person) issue in practical obedience to Jesus; but in itself it is simply the recognition of the divinely given authority of Jesus Christ to rule over man as exalted Lord, and the personal acknowledgement of oneself as under that authority. If we may quote Ladd's comment again, the Christian convert, by means of this confession (and the repentance which it expresses), 'has entered into a new relationship in which he acknowledges the absolute sovereignty and mastery of the exalted Jesus over his life'.[43]

Admittedly, many people have become Christians without making this acknowledgement explicit, or perhaps without even understanding it or its implications.

Yet it must be regarded as a biblical requirement that there be found in the convert's thinking at least the implicit acknowledgement of Jesus' rightful authority over himself; the New Testament teaching can mean no less than this. In other words, no one can be truly converted while rejecting the lordship of Jesus Christ.

In the second place, the objection we are now considering manifests a faulty view of the nature of 'saving faith', biblically understood. 'Faith' or 'believing' in the Bible rarely means the mere acknowledgement of historical fact,[44] but also includes the embracing of the God who stands behind those facts, as well as the change of mind described above. In other words, faith implies repentance and personal trust. It is not a matter of faith *plus* repentance; rather, faith *includes* repentance. This is demonstrated by the regularity with which *metanoeō* ('to repent') and *metanoia* ('repentance') occur in Acts, sometimes standing alone to express the appropriate response of man to the gospel (Acts 2:38; 3:19; 5:31; 8:22; 11:18; 17:30; 20:21, significant as Paul's own summary of his three-year ministry at Ephesus; 26:20). J. Behm correctly observes that 'according to Acts the heart of the apostolic mission is the message of *metanoia*,' a *metanoia* to be rendered particularly in the light of Jesus' exaltation to lordship.[45]

Repentance occurs earlier in New Testament preaching as well. It is the predominant note in the preaching of John the Baptist, where it has clear moral implications (Matt. 3:2, 8, etc.).[46] Repentance is also the hallmark of Jesus' proclamation, as recorded by Mark: 'The time is fulfilled, and the kingdom of God is at hand; repent and believe in the gospel' (Mark 1:15). The whole of Jesus' ministry is characterized by the demand for repentance, expressed in the strongest terms.[47]

It will not do to regard repentance as possessing a peculiar dispensational or 'kingdom' application relevant only to Jews,[48] nor can it be reduced to the mere acknowledgement of Jesus' deity.[49] It is required by God of all men (Acts 17:30), has definite moral implications (Acts 26:20), and is an integral part of the preaching of the gospel (Acts 20:21) and of the believing response which God seeks (Acts 2:38). As expressed in the oft-quoted statement of John Murray, 'The faith that is unto salvation is a penitent faith and the repentance that is unto life is a believing repentance . . . It is impossible to disentangle faith and repentance.'[50] We conclude that there is inherent within biblically defined 'saving faith' a change of attitude known as 'repentance', a change which is roughly equivalent to acknowledging in principle the rightful authority (or lordship) of Jesus Christ over oneself.

2.    Another objection which must be considered is that there are instances in the Bible of known Christians (or Old Testament believers) who were not always submissive to the lordship of Christ, thus demonstrating that such submission is not essential to one's justification. Ryrie adduces the examples of Peter (in Acts 10:14), Barnabas (Acts 15:39), the Ephesian converts who formerly practised magic (Acts 19: 18–19), and Lot (in Genesis) as exhibiting various degrees of being unyielded to the lordship of Christ.[51] Harrison also mentions Peter (Matt. 16:22; Acts 10:14), adding that Peter 'certainly was not making Christ Lord on these occasions'.[52]

In the first place, it may be noted that the Bible never uses language such as Harrison does here. The Christian does not 'make Christ Lord', nor is he ever urged to do so. Rather, God has made Jesus Lord (Acts 2:36), and those who hear the gospel are called upon to acknowledge His lordship.

In the second place, the New Testament never expresses the expectation that the Christian's submission to the lordship of Jesus will in fact be perfect. Full submission and obedience are certainly desirable, and are the goal that is set before Christians, but the New Testament throughout recognizes that the believer will continue to sin and to need forgiveness (e.g., the Lord's prayer, Matt. 6:12; 1 John 1:8—2:2). This objection thus constitutes another instance of confusing the Christian's acknowledgement in principle of the lordship of Jesus with the practical observance of that lordship. The confession that Jesus is Lord involves acknowledging His rightful sovereignty over the believer; it is not a declaration that the Christian will be perfect from that point forward. Never is it pretended, in Scripture or in a biblical Christian theology, that the believer will always render absolute and perfect obedience to his Lord. It is growth in the Christian life that leads the believer into greater and greater degrees of holiness and practical submission to the Lord Jesus.

This objection, expressed in its simplest form, is that Christians sin. The fact is readily granted (although Ryrie's examples are not particularly persuasive).[53] But an instance of sin, or even a prolonged period of backsliding, does not, in biblical terms, constitute a rejection or invalidation of the principle of Christ's lordship over the believer; it simply constitutes disobedience to one's Lord. The relationship of the believer to Jesus Christ as a subject/servant to his Lord is an objective one; it does not change. The subject/servant may be more or less obedient to his Lord, but his obedience or disobedience is always rendered in relation to the One who is his Lord.

Ryrie's use of this argument is not only faulty, but it can also be used against his own position. In the last chapter of his book he expounds his own view of 'The Balanced Christian Life'.[54] At the heart of true spirituality (he believes) is an experience he calls 'dedication', in which the believer makes a 'complete, crisis commitment of self for all the years of one's life'.[55] The question arises, 'What is the situation when a Christian who has "dedicated" himself to Christ falls into sin?' Is he to be regarded as no longer (or perhaps never) 'dedicated'? Ryrie would appear not to think so, for he considers the period after 'dedication' to be one of growth and gradual maturation, not one of perfection.[56] Yet he argues that the confession 'Jesus is [my] Lord' is rendered invalid if the confessor later falls into sin. He does not appear willing to recognize the fact (in this case) that the practical implementation of the rightful claims of the Lord Jesus is a gradual and growing process. Ryrie's objection is as applicable to his own position as to that which he opposes; it must be regarded as valid for both or as valid for neither. It seems to this writer that the latter is the case.

Related to this objection is another, offered by Harrison, to the effect that requiring the confession of

Jesus' lordship 'rules out the necessity for large portions of the practical teaching of the epistles'.[57] In other words, if Christians are already submitted to the lordship of Christ, why should they be further urged to submit? At the risk of becoming repetitious, it must once again be said that this objection confuses the principle and the practice of the lordship of Jesus. The practical exhortations of the New Testament do not urge Christians to make an initial acknowledgement of Jesus' lordship; it is assumed that they have already done so. Rather, Christians are urged to render practical daily obedience to Jesus who is their Lord. Indeed, it is precisely on the basis of Jesus' acknowledged lordship over believers that obedience is enjoined: 'As you therefore have received Christ Jesus the Lord [NIV: 'as Lord'], so walk in Him' (Col. 2:6). The practical portions of the New Testament show the believer how the lordship of Jesus is to be manifested in daily life. Harrison's objection is thus seen to be without substance.

3. A further major objection, advanced by Ryrie, is that requiring of converts the confession that 'Jesus is Lord' leaves no room for the 'carnal Christian'. He asks, 'If only committed people are saved people, then where is there room for carnal Christians?'[58]

A proper response to this objection must be made on two levels. In the first place, if the objection suggests that the confession 'Jesus is Lord' demands perfection of the believer in order for him to be regarded as truly a Christian, then the objection is not valid. The confession of Jesus' lordship does not promote a form of perfectionism. We have already noted this above. The acknowledgement of the principle of Jesus' lordship is not rendered invalid by the Christian's failure to achieve absolute submission and total obedience to the Lord Jesus. Growth in submission and obedience is the task of a lifetime.

But in the second place, if this objection intends to say that requiring the acknowledgement of the principle of Jesus' sovereignty over the believer allows no room for what is popularly known as the 'carnal Christian' — a professing Christian who shows no practical evidence of conversion — then the objection is correct. The biblical view of conversion and the practical implications of confessing Jesus' lordship are incompatible with the commonly held theory of the 'carnal Christian'.

The New Testament speaks of the Christian as one who has made a definitive break with the ruling power of sin, as one who has experienced a radical God-ward reorientation of his life. One of the most compelling scriptural passages to set forth this view of the believer is Romans 6. Paul in this chapter describes the Christian as one who has experienced a radical break with the dominion of sin. 'Our old self,' Paul says, 'was crucified with Him . . . that we should no longer be slaves to sin' (Rom. 6:6). Just as Christ died to sin once for all and is now alive unto God, so should the believer regard himself, by virtue of his union with Christ in his death and resurrection (6:8—11). The practical exhortation of verses 12—13 is based on this truth; the Christian is called upon to live in accordance with what he is in fact. This is further emphasized by verse 14, which says that 'sin shall not be master over you, for you are not under law, but under grace'. It is instructive to note that the word translated 'be master over' is *kyrieuō*, a verb of the *kyrios* word-group meaning 'be lord or master, rule, control'.[59] The force of Paul's statement is that sin will in fact no longer be 'lord' or 'master' over the Christian; its dominion has been broken. The Christian has exchanged one 'lord' (sin) for another (Christ). This understanding of the chapter is confirmed by verses 15—23, in which believers are described by means of a series of contrasts between their old life and their new. Christians once were 'slaves of sin' (v. 17) but have become 'slaves of righteousness' (v. 18). They have been 'freed from [the slavery of] sin and enslaved to God' (v. 22). These terms describe a definite and permanent change of masters in the Christian's life.[60]

The same sharply drawn portrait of the Christian is found in the First Epistle of John. 'The one who says, "I have come to know Him", and does not keep His commandments, is a liar, and the truth is not in him' (1 John 2:4). This black-and-white picture of the believer characterizes the whole Epistle (see 1:6; 2:9; 3:6—10; 4:8, 20; 5:18), and speaks not of the Christian's sinlessness (cf. 1:8—2:2) but of a definitive break with the ruling power of sin in his life.

This biblical view of the Christian contrasts sharply with the theory of the 'carnal Christian'. This term, as commonly used, describes a professing Christian who shows little or no evidence of having been truly converted; he approaches the state of being totally and permanently carnal (meaning unspiritual, unsanctified). The term 'carnal' derives from the King James Version's rendering of 1 Corinthians 3:1—3, where it translates *sarkinos* (v. 1) and *sarkikos* (v. 3), both meaning 'belonging to the realm of the flesh'.[61] This passage is often appealed to in support of the 'carnal Christian' theory, but it should be noted that Paul is here dealing with a single particular sin of the Corinthian church (divisiveness), and on that basis alone calls them 'carnal'. There is certainly no ground here, nor elsewhere in the New Testament, for regarding as a genuine Christian believer one who is in a constant and total state of carnality. Yet that is what is demanded by the 'carnal Christian' theory. One widely used booklet describes the 'carnal' Christian as manifesting the following qualities: controlled by self, discouragement, self-seeking, doubt, a critical spirit, defeat, wrong doctrine, frustration, aimlessness, envy, worry, jealousy, impure thoughts, a legalistic life, a poor prayer life and a fruitless witness for Christ.[62] The question might arise in the minds of some readers of the New Testament, 'Where is there any biblical basis for considering such a person a Christian at all?' This list is strikingly similar in some of its elements to Paul's catalogue of 'the deeds of the flesh' in Galatians 5:19—21, concerning which he says that 'those who practise such things shall not inherit the kingdom of God'. There indeed seems to be little room in the New Testament for the 'carnal Christian'. Rather, for the Christian, the New Testament teaches, the dominion of sin has been replaced by the lordship of Jesus Christ.[63]

4. There are several miscellaneous objections which may be treated briefly together. Harrison argues that 'this position is unsupported by the examples of

gospel preaching in the book of Acts'.[64] For support of this assertion he appeals to Acts 2:38, which contains a call to repentance following immediately upon the announcement of Jesus' exaltation and lordship (Acts 2:32—36). Clearly, this passage does not support Harrison's position; rather, it refutes it. Admittedly, Acts does not contain the specific language that Harrison demands, that is, that people be 'pressed to acknowledge Jesus Christ as their personal Lord in order to be saved,' but that is simply because the apostles speak in different terms than those of Harrison's formula. They proclaim the death, exaltation and lordship of Jesus and call for repentance and faith (see above, pp. 54—58, 74). In different terms, Acts affirms what Harrison denies.

Harrison also argues that 'the ground of assurance of salvation is endangered if surrender to Christ's lordship is a part of that ground'.[65] As Harrison pursues this argument, it becomes clear that he regards perfect and constant obedience to be the criterion of 'surrender to Christ's lordship', a standard to which no Christian will attain. This manifests once again a confusion between the principle and the practice of Christ's lordship, and what has already been said on this matter applies here as well. It should be noted, however, that while the ground of the believer's *justification* before God is the righteousness of Christ, the ground of his *assurance* of salvation does include his own practical holiness (see 1 John 2:3, 5—6; 3:14, 18—20; and the passages in 1 John mentioned above, p. 81). In this respect, Harrison is objecting to something which is thoroughly biblical.

Ryrie attempts to demonstrate that *kyrios* when applied to Jesus simply means 'God', and that to confess Jesus as Lord is only to acknowledge His deity.[66] This position cannot be sustained by the evidence. The implication of legitimate authority inheres in the word *kyrios* (see Chapter 1) and it is so used both in the Septuagint and throughout the New Testament. Ryrie's approach ignores Jesus' mediatorial lordship (see Chapter 2), and is refuted by a single sentence in the New Testament, Thomas' confession of Jesus as 'my Lord and my God' (John 20:28), in which 'Lord' must clearly mean something other than simply 'God'.

Finally, Ryrie charges that to require the confession of Jesus' lordship confuses salvation with discipleship.[67] But Ryrie's treatment of the gospel passages dealing with discipleship is unconvincing; while the concepts of discipleship and salvation may be distinguished, Jesus never intended to separate the two. Ryrie thus fails to grasp the true meaning of Jesus' teaching in such passages as Luke 14:25—35. Jesus here affirms that in coming to Him one enters a life of discipleship, a life in which Jesus' legitimate and absolute claim on the convert and his possessions must be acknowledged. In light of this fact, Jesus says, it is best for the would-be follower to count the cost. 'There could be no following', as John Stott puts it, 'without a forsaking, a renunciation (in principle if not in literal fact) of competing loyalties, of family relationships, of personal ambitions, of material possessions.'[68] Furthermore, Ryrie's position is positively refuted by such a passage as Matthew 11:28—30. Here Jesus invites His hearers both to 'come to Me' and to 'take My yoke upon you and learn of Me,' with the promise of 'rest' connected with both these elements, binding them into an indivisible unity. The verb translated 'learn' is *manthanō* (related to *mathētēs*, 'learner' or 'disciple'), and the aorist imperative 'indicates the decisive step of *becoming* a disciple, of *entering* His school, of *acknowledging* Him as our Teacher and Lord'. There is found in this passage, Stott rightly says, 'the true balance of the gospel. Jesus offers us both rest and a yoke'.[69]

# 4

# The practical significance of the confession of Jesus as Lord

It remains for us to consider some of the practical implications of the biblical pattern of proclaiming and confessing Jesus Christ as Lord. The immediately clear and obvious implication is that twentieth-century evangelicals, as modern heirs of the apostolic tradition, are obligated to adhere as closely as possible to that biblical pattern of proclamation and confession which has been handed down to them. In practical terms, this suggests that we ourselves must confess Jesus as Lord, that we must proclaim to the world that Jesus is Lord, and that we must seek from those whom we evangelize the acknowledgement that Jesus is Lord. But it is evident that such is not the uniform conviction or practice within present-day evangelicalism. There is widespread confusion regarding the nature and content of the gospel, and equally widespread deviation from the pattern of preaching and evangelism found in the New Testament. The present writer wishes to address this situation by posing some questions concerning the practical results of such deviation, and then by suggesting some positive ways in which the biblical pattern may be restored.

## Results of ignoring the lordship of Jesus in preaching and evangelism

That modern evangelicalism has to a considerable degree failed to reflect the biblical pattern as set forth in the present study needs no elaborate demonstration; the view advocated by Harrison and Ryrie is very popular. But could there not be some serious practical consequences of such a failure? The following questions suggest what are perhaps some of the weightier of these.

*1.* By ignoring the lordship of Jesus in preaching and evangelism, are we not fostering a superficial and man-centred form of evangelism which could result in false conversions and in a false sense of assurance among those who are so 'converted'?

This is by far the most serious and disturbing question to be raised here, but it is one which must be faced. If we dilute or alter the biblical message, then it is inevitable that the gospel will be proclaimed erroneously. And if proclaimed erroneously, could it not be received erroneously? By ignoring or eliminating the biblical emphasis on the lordship of Jesus, and the necessity for confessing that lordship, could we not be deluding those who hear our message, by (i) offering to them a salvation which is radically different from the biblical concept (which involves man's right attitude towards God as well as his formal standing before God), and by (ii) offering to them salvation on terms other than those on which God Himself offers it (repentant faith, not a so-called 'faith' which is devoid of repentance)? And what of those who receive our message? Could we not be deceiving them into thinking that they have fulfilled the biblical conditions of salvation (if such a term can properly be used) and that they are secure in Christ, when in fact they have not and are not? And are not such people in a worse spiritual condition after such 'believing' than they were before?

There are recent indications that such questions are not inappropriate. In the September 1977 issue of *Eternity*, C. Peter Wagner published the results of a survey taken in the aftermath of the 'Here's Life America' evangelistic campaign sponsored by Campus Crusade for Christ in 1976. In the six metropolitan areas where the survey was conducted, the 178 participating churches reported 26,535 gospel presentations and 4,106 'decisions for Christ', of which 525 joined follow-up Bible studies and 125 became church members.[1] In other words, 3 per cent of the 'converts' joined Christian churches. When judged on the basis of Wagner's premise that evangelistic results should be reflected in church growth, and even allowing for various extenuating factors, this is a dismal record. What became of the rest? What is their spiritual condition? It would appear that something is drastically wrong here. Is it not worth considering the possibility that the problem may be as much one of faulty theology as it is one of faulty methodology?

2. By minimizing the lordship of Jesus in preaching and evangelism, and thus at the point of conversion, are we not fostering a faulty view of sin and of the necessity for sanctification on the part of Christians?

The Bible describes the Christian as one who has experienced a definitive break with the ruling power of sin (see above, pp. 80–82). To eliminate the necessity for the lordship of Jesus in the Christian's life is to deny this truth. Not only could this denial lead to a faulty understanding of the Christian life in general, but could it not also serve to obliterate the primary observable distinction between Christians and non-Christians — which is that the Christian is one who has given himself to live in obedience to the Lord Jesus? What is there that visibly distinguishes the believer from the unbeliever, apart from submission to the lordship of Jesus Christ?

It may be instructive in this regard to consider the matter of the 'carnal Christian'. It is difficult to avoid the suspicion that there is more than just a casual connection between the 'carnal Christian' theory and the faulty evangelism illustrated above. Could it be, as John Sanderson suggests, that 'the permanently carnal Christian is a figment of the imagination, invented to accommodate a certain doctrinal viewpoint'?[2] Invented, perhaps, to explain 'converts' who show no sign of being converted at all? Would it not be more biblical to acknowledge the basic truth, as expressed again by Sanderson, that 'one may (and we all do) have carnal moments, but the Christian must have meaningful character growth, or else he is not a Christian'?[3]

3. By relegating the acknowledgement of Jesus' lordship to a later point in the Christian life, are we not encouraging Christians to seek an unbiblical 'second blessing' or crisis experience of God's grace or of commitment to Him?

Whether such a second experience be called 'making Jesus Lord of one's life', or 'becoming a disciple', or 'dedication', or 'entering the victorious life', or being 'baptized with the Spirit' — the list could go on — is it not essentially an unscriptural experience that is being encouraged and sought, and does not the whole effort constitute a denial of the biblical teaching which regards all of these — biblically defined — as taking place at the time of conversion? It is strange that men who strongly repudiate many of the unscriptural elements in the so-called 'charismatic movement' actually espouse a theology that in essence amounts to the same thing — that being 'in Christ' is not sufficient, that there must be some further crisis experience in order for the Christian to receive all that God intends for him. Kenneth L. Gentry has documented the affinities between the teaching of those who advocate a second crisis experience of dedication, lordship or disciple-ship and that of the 'victorious life' movement of the late nineteenth and early twentieth centuries;[4] its similarity to certain aspects of current 'charismatic' teaching is also evident.

## Suggested correctives for evangelical preaching and evangelism

These questions lead to the further question: 'What must we do to restore the biblical pattern of proclaiming and confessing Jesus as Lord?' The present writer offers the following suggestions.

*1.* We must preach the apostolic gospel in its fullness. That means proclaiming the resurrection, exaltation and lordship of Jesus Christ as well as His death. It is difficult, in the light of what we have seen in Acts, to imagine the apostles preaching the latter apart from the former; and yet our modern tendency is to do so, emphasizing the death of Jesus while ignoring His exaltation. Geoffrey Wilson has well said that 'no preaching which fails to do justice to Christ's present sovereignty is faithful to the authoritative pattern laid down in the New Testament'.[5] The gospel includes *all* the 'good news' of what God has wrought through Jesus Christ.

2.   We must give due emphasis to the necessity and meaning of acknowledging Jesus as Lord. In evangelism this means that we must not dilute the biblical demand for repentance (Acts 17:30), nor must we fail to explain the significance of the confession of Jesus' lordship (Rom. 10:9; see above pp. 65–70). This may result in fewer 'decisions', but it will promote genuine conversions.

3.   We need to reformulate some of our teaching concerning the Christian life, in particular that teaching which deals with the various 'crisis experiences' through which Christians may pass. It would seem that a more biblical terminology than that which is commonly used could be developed. Kenneth Prior makes a helpful attempt to do so in his volume, *The Way of Holiness.*[6] He suggests that while some supposed experiences of a 'second blessing' may actually amount to initial conversion, other experiences (popularly described by the various terms mentioned above, including 'making Christ Lord of one's life') may be regarded as perhaps one or another of the following: recovery from backsliding, the discovery of some neglected scriptural truth, a sudden awareness of the cost of discipleship,

gaining 'full assurance' of one's salvation, experiencing God's special guidance or exercising certain gifts of the Holy Spirit. On the whole, this seems an eminently more scriptural approach than that of emphasizing the necessity of some such experience as 'making Christ Lord', 'dedication', 'discipleship', etc., as is commonly done.

*4.* Finally, we must offer a living demonstration of that to which we call our hearers — a willing submission to the authority of Jesus Christ as Lord. It is only when our words are supported by our actions that they will carry conviction and power. It must be true of us even as we press the truth upon others: Jesus is Lord.

# Appendix

*1. Theanthropic constitution.* From the time of conception in the womb of the virgin, and for ever, the second Person of the Godhead is God-man. This identity did not suffer dissolution even in death. The death meant separation of the elements of His human nature. But He, as the Son of God, was still united to the two separated elements of His human nature. He, as respects His body, was laid in the tomb and, as respects His disembodied spirit, He went to the Father. He was buried. He was raised from the dead. He was indissolubly united to the disunited elements of His human nature. When He was raised from the dead, human nature in its restored integrity belonged to His person, and it was in that restored integrity that He manifested Himself repeatedly to His disciples and to various other persons, including more than five hundred at one time. It was in this human nature that He ascended to heaven and sat down at the right hand of God. It is as God-man He is exalted and given all authority in heaven and in earth. It is in human nature that He will return, and as God-man He will judge the world. The elect will be conformed to His image, and it is as the firstborn among many brethren that He will fulfil the Father's predestinating design (Rom. 8:29; cf. Phil. 3:21). The thought of ceasing to be the God-man is, therefore, alien to all that the Scripture reveals respecting His own glory and the glory of those for whose sake He became man.

*2. Economic subordination.* By the incarnation and by taking the form of a Servant, the Son came to sustain new relations to the Father and the Holy Spirit. He became subject to the Father and dependent upon the operations of the Holy Spirit. He came down from heaven, not to do His own will, but the will of the Father who sent Him (cf. John 6:38). As the Father had life in Himself, so gave He to the Son to have life in Himself (cf. John 5:26). It is in this light that we are to interpret Jesus' statement, 'The Father is greater than I' (John 14:28). It is our Lord's servanthood that advertises this subordination more than any other office. As servant He was obedient unto death (cf. Phil. 2:7, 8).

Manifold were the activities of the Holy Spirit. By the Spirit He was begotten in Mary's womb. With the Spirit He was endued at the baptism in Jordan. By the Spirit He was driven into the wilderness to be tempted of the devil. In the power of the Spirit He returned to Galilee. By the Spirit He cast out demons. In the Holy Spirit He rejoiced and gave thanks (cf. Luke 10:21). Through the eternal Spirit He offered Himself and fulfilled the climactic demand of His commission (cf. Heb. 9:12). According to the Spirit He was constituted the Son of God with power in the resurrection (cf. Rom. 1:4). By virtue of this, Christ is 'life-giving Spirit'

(1 Cor. 15:45), and Paul can say, 'The Lord is the Spirit' (2 Cor. 3:17). He is given the Spirit without measure (cf. John 3:34).

*3. Mediatorial investiture.* The authority with which He is invested as a result of His obedience unto death must be distinguished from the authority and government that He possesses and exercises intrinsically as God the Son. The latter is intrinsic to His deity (cf. Matt. 28:18; John 3:35; Acts 2:36; Eph. 1:20—23; Phil. 2:9—11; 1 Peter 3:22). This authority and sovereignty is universal and all-inclusive. How it is related to the sovereignty that is intrinsic we cannot tell. Here is another aspect of the duality that exists all along the line in the mystery of the incarnation. The duality in this instance consists in the coexistence of the exercise of prerogatives belonging to Him in virtue of His Godhood and of prerogatives which were bestowed upon Him as Mediator and Lord. Mystery enshrouds this duality for us, but we may not deny the coexistence or the distinctions involved.

# Bibliography

Abbott, T. K., *A Critical and Exegetical Commentary on the Epistles to the Ephesians and to the Colossians,* International Critical Commentary, Edinburgh: T. & T. Clark, 1897.

Aland, Kurt, Black, M., Martini, C. M., Metzger, B. M., and Wikgren, A., eds., *The Greek New Testament,* 3rd ed., New York: American Bible Society, 1975.

Alexander, Joseph Addison, *A Commentary on the Acts of the Apostles,* 2 vols in 1, Reprint ed. London: Banner of Truth Trust, 1963.

Arndt, William F., and Gingrich, F. Wilbur, *A Greek-English Lexicon of the New Testament and Other Early Christian Literature,* A translation and adaptation of the fourth revised and augmented edition of Walter Bauer's *Griechisch-Deutsches Wörterbuch zu den Schriften des Neuen Testaments . . .* Second edition revised and augmented by F. Wilbur Gingrich and Frederick W. Danker from Walter Bauer's fifth edition, 1958, Chicago: University of Chicago Press, 1979.

Berkhof, Louis, *Systematic Theology,* Reprint ed., Edinburgh: Banner of Truth Trust, 1974.

Broadus, John A., 'Commentary on the Gospel of Matthew' in Alvah Hovey, ed., *An American Commentary on the New Testament,* 7 vols., Valley Forge: American Baptist Publication Society, 1886, Vol. 1.

Brown, Colin, gen. ed., *The New International Dictionary of New Testament Theology,* Translated from the German *Theologisches Begriffslexicon zum Neuen Testament,* 3 vols., Grand Rapids: Zondervan, 1975—78.

Bruce, F. F., *The Epistle of Paul to the Romans,* Tyndale New Testament Commentaries, Grand Rapids: Eerdmans, 1963..

Bruce, F. F., *The Epistle to the Ephesians,* Westwood, N. J.: Fleming H. Revell Co., 1961.

Chafer, Lewis Sperry, *Systematic Theology,* 8 vols., Dallas: Dallas Seminary Press, 1947.

Cranfield, C. E. B., *A Critical and Exegetical Commentary on the Epistle to the Romans,* International Critical Commentary, 2 vols., Edinburgh: T. & T. Clark, 1975, 1979.

Cullmann, Oscar, *The Christology of the New Testament,* Translated by Shirley C. Guthrie and Charles A. M. Hall, rev. ed., Philadelphia: Westminster Press, 1963.

Cullmann, Oscar, *The Earliest Christian Confessions,* Translated by J. K. S. Reid, London: Lutterworth Press, 1949.

Douglas, J. D., ed., *The New Bible Dictionary,* Grand Rapids: Eerdmans, 1962.

Gentry, Kenneth L., 'The Great Option: A Study of the Lordship Controversy', *Baptist Reformation Review* 5 (Spring 1976): 49—79.

Ginter, Marlene, and Trax, Karen, 'Is Jesus Christ the Lord of Your Life?' *Baptist Herald*, February, 1978, p. 12.

*A Handy Concordance to the Septuagint*, Reprint ed., London: Samuel Bagster & Sons, 1970.

Harrison, Everett F., 'Must Christ Be Lord To Be Savior? No', *Eternity*, September 1959, p. 14.

Harrison, E. F., 'Romans' in Frank E. Gaebelein, ed., *The Expositor's Bible Commentary*, 12 vols. (incomplete), Grand Rapids: Zondervan, 1976-, 10:1—171.

*'Have You Made the Wonderful Discovery of the Spirit-Filled Life?'* Campus Crusade for Christ, 1966.

Hendriksen, William, *Exposition of Ephesians*, New Testament Commentary, Grand Rapids: Baker Book House, 1967.

Hendriksen, William, *Exposition of Philippians*, New Testament Commentary, Grand Rapids: Baker Book House, 1962.

Hodge, Charles, *A Commentary on Romans*, Reprint ed., London: Banner of Truth Trust, 1972.

Hodge, Charles, *Commentary on the Epistle to the Ephesians*, Reprinted, Old Tappan, N.J., Fleming H. Revell Co.

Hoeksema, Herman, *Reformed Dogmatics*, Grand Rapids: Reformed Free Publishing Association, 1966.

*Holy Bible: New International Version*, Grand Rapids: Zondervan, 1978.

Hughes, Philip Edgcumbe, *Paul's Second Epistle to the Corinthians,* New International Commentary on the New Testament, Grand Rapids: Eerdmans, 1962.

Kittel, Gerhard, and Friedrich, Gerhard, eds., *Theological Dictionary of the New Testament,* Translated and edited by Geoffrey W. Bromiley, 10 vols., Grand Rapids: Eerdmans, 1964–76.

Ladd, George Eldon, *A Theology of the New Testament,* Grand Rapids: Eerdmans, 1974.

Lange, John Peter, *Commentary on the Holy Scriptures: Critical, Doctrinal and Homiletical,* Translated and edited by Philip Schaff, 24 vols. in 12, Reprint ed., Grand Rapids: Zondervan, 1960.

Liddell, Henry George, and Scott, Robert. *A Greek-English Lexicon,* Revised by Henry Stuart Jones, with supplement, Oxford: Oxford University Press, 1968.

Lightfoot, J. B., *Saint Paul's Epistle to the Philippians,* London: Macmillan, 1891.

Lloyd-Jones, D. Martyn, *Romans: An Exposition of Chapter 6,* London: Banner of Truth Trust, 1972.

Martin, R. P., *Carmen Christi: Philippians 2:5–11 in Recent Interpretation and in the Setting of Early Christian Worship,* Cambridge: Cambridge University Press, 1967.

Morris, Leon, *The Gospel According to John,* New International Commentary on the New Testament, Grand Rapids: Eerdmans, 1971.

Motyer, J. A., *Philippian Studies: The Richness of Christ,* Chicago: Inter-Varsity Press, 1966.

Moule, C. F. D., *The Origin of Christology,* Cambridge: Cambridge University Press, 1977.

Moulton, W. F., and Geden, A. S., eds. *A Concordance to the Greek Testament*, 4th ed., Edited by H. K. Moulton, Edinburgh: T. & T. Clark, 1963.

Mounce, Robert H., *The Essential Nature of New Testament Preaching*, Grand Rapids: Eerdmans, 1960.

Murray, John, *Collected Writings of John Murray*, Vol. 2, Edinburgh: Banner of Truth Trust, 1977.

Murray, John, *The Epistle to the Romans*, New International Commentary on the New Testament, 2 vols in 1, Grand Rapids: Eerdmans, 1959, 1965.

Murray, John, *Redemption Accomplished and Applied*, Grand Rapids: Eerdmans, 1955.

Needham, David C., *Birthright: Christian, Do you know who you are?*, Portland, Oregon: Multnomah Press, 1979.

Nestle, Eberhard, and Aland, Kurt and Barbara, *Novum Testamentum Graece*, 26th ed., Stuttgart: Deutsche Bibelstiftung, 1979.

Neufeld, Vernon H., *The Earliest Christian Confessions*, Grand Rapids: Eerdmans, 1963.

*New American Standard Bible*, Philadelphia: A. J. Holman Company, 1973.

Nicoll, W. Robertson, ed., *The Expositor's Greek Testament*, 5 vols, Reprint ed., Grand Rapids: Eerdmans, 1967.

Prior, Kenneth F. W., *The Way of Holiness*, London: Inter-Varsity Press, 1967.

Rahlfs, Alfred, ed., *Septuaginta*, 2 vols., 9th ed., Stuttgart: Württembergische Bibelanstalt, 1971.

Reisinger, Ernest C., *What Should We Think of 'The Carnal Christian'?*, Edinburgh: Banner of Truth Trust.

Ridderbos, Herman, *Paul: An Outline of His Theology*, Translated by John Richard De Witt, Grand Rapids: Eerdmans, 1975.

Robinson, J. Armitage, *St Paul's Epistle to the Ephesians*, London: James Clarke & Co.

Ryrie, Charles Caldwell, *Balancing the Christian Life*, Chicago: Moody Press, 1969.

Sanderson, John W., *The Fruit of the Spirit*, Grand Rapids: Zondervan, 1972.

Shedd, W. G. T., *Dogmatic Theology*, 3 vols, Reprint ed., Grand Rapids: Zondervan, 1969.

Stott, John R., 'Must Christ Be Lord To Be Savior? Yes', *Eternity*, September 1959, p. 15.

Vos, Geerhardus, *The Self-Disclosure of Jesus*, Edited by Johannes G. Vos, Phillipsburg, N. J. : Presbyterian and Reformed Publishing Co., 1978.

Wagner, C. Peter, 'Who Found It?', *Eternity*, September 1977, pp. 13—19.

Warfield, Benjamin Breckinridge, *Perfectionism*, Edited by Samuel G. Craig, Philadelphia: Presbyterian and Reformed Publishing Co., 1974.

Westcott, Brooke Foss, *Saint Paul's Epistle to the Ephesians*, Reprint ed., Minneapolis: Klock & Klock Christian Publishers, 1978.

Wilson, Geoffrey B., *Romans: A Digest of Reformed Comment*, Rev. ed., Edinburgh: Banner of Truth Trust, 1977.

# Notes

Intro.

[1] Everett F. Harrison, 'Must Christ Be Lord To Be Savior? No,' *Eternity*, September 1959, p. 14; John R. Stott, 'Must Christ Be Lord To Be Savior? Yes,' *Eternity*, September 1959, p. 15.

[2] Charles Caldwell Ryrie, *Balancing the Christian Life* (Chicago: Moody Press, 1969), pp. 169—81.

[3] Ryrie, p. 170.

[4] Everett F. Harrison, 'Romans', in *The Expositor's Bible Commentary*, ed. Frank E. Gaebelein, vol. 10 (Grand Rapids: Zondervan, 1976), p. 112.

[5] Marlene Ginter and Karen Trax, 'Is Jesus Christ the Lord of Your Life?' *Baptist Herald*, February 1978, p. 12.

Ch. 1

[1] The following summary is based on the article on *kyrios* by W. Foerster and G. Quell in vol. 3 of G. Kittel and G. Friedrich, eds., *Theological Dictionary of the New Testament*, trans. and ed. Geoffrey W. Bromiley, 10 vols. (Grand Rapids: Eerdmans, 1964—76), pp. 1039—98; and that on 'Lord' by H. Bietenhard in vol. 2 of Colin Brown, gen. ed., *The New International Dictionary of New Testament Theology*, translated from the German *Theologisches Begriffslexicon zum Neuen Testament*, 3 vols. (Grand Rapids: Zondervan, 1975—78), pp. 508—20; and supplemented by additional sources. The Kittel and Brown dictionaries will hereinafter be referred to as *TDNT* and *NIDNTT* respectively.

[2] Henry George Liddell and Robert Scott, *A Greek-English Lexicon*, rev. Henry Stuart Jones, with supplement (Oxford: Oxford University Press, 1968), pp. 1013–14.

[3] *NIDNTT*, 2:510.

[4] *TDNT*, 3:1042–43.

[5] *TDNT*, 3:1043.

[6] *TDNT*, 3:1045.

[7] *TDNT*, 3:1048.

[8] *TDNT*, 3:1048.

[9] *TDNT*, 3:1049.

[10] *TDNT*, 3:1051.

[11] *TDNT*, 3:1051.

[12] *TDNT*, 3:1052.

[13] *TDNT*, 3:1052.

[14] *TDNT*, 3:1054–58; *NIDNTT*, 2:510–11.

[15] For a treatment of this question see Oscar Cullmann, *The Christology of the New Testament*, trans. Shirley C. Guthrie and Charles A. M. Hall, revised edition (Philadelphia: Westminster Press, 1963), pp. 195–199.

[16] *NIDNTT*, 2:512.

[17] William F. Arndt and F. Wilbur Gingrich, *A Greek-English Lexicon of the New Testament and Other Early Christian Literature* (a translation and adaptation of the fourth revised and augmented edition of Walter Bauer's *Griechisch-Deutsches Wörterbuch zu den Schriften des Neuen Testaments . . .*), second edition revised and augmented by F. Wilbur Gingrich and Frederick W. Danker from Walter Bauer's fifth edition (Chicago: University of Chicago Press, 1979), p. 459. Hereinafter referred to as Arndt-Gingrich-Danker.

[18] Geerhardus Vos, *The Self-Disclosure of Jesus*, ed. Johannes G. Vos (Phillipsburg, N. J. : Presbyterian and Reformed Publishing Co., 1978), p. 118.

[19] Vos, p. 121.

[20] Vos, p. 127.

[21] Vos, p. 135.

[22] Vos, pp. 135–36.
[23] Vos, p. 136.

Ch. 2

[1] Arndt-Gingrich-Danker, p. 850.

[2] While it is possible that the phrase *tē dexia* ('the right hand') has in Acts 2:33 and 5:31 an instrumental sense ('by the right hand'), the weight of New Testament usage would favour a locative sense ('at the right hand'). For the meaning of this phrase see below, p.

[3] See Arndt-Gingrich-Danker, p. 850; *TDNT*, 8:610; Leon Morris, *The Gospel According to John,* New International Commentary on the New Testament (Grand Rapids: Eerdmans, 1971), pp. 225–26.

[4] See R. P. Martin, *Carmen Christi: Philippians 2:5–11 in Recent Interpretation and in the Setting of Early Christian Worship* (Cambridge: Cambridge University Press, 1967), pp. 63–95.

[5] George Eldon Ladd, *A Theology of the New Testament* (Grand Rapids: Eerdmans, 1974), p. 416. See also Martin, p. 244.

[6] See Martin's discussion of Käsemann's view, p. 238.

[7] 'It is difficult to understand how authority could be committed to the Son which was not properly His in His own right.' Lewis Sperry Chafer, *Systematic Theology,* 8 vols. (Dallas: Dallas Seminary Press, 1947), 5:274.

[8] Arndt-Gingrich-Danker, p. 876.

[9] Martin, p. 245. Martin lists in a lengthy note on page 245 several interpreters who favour this identification, to which may be added, Ladd, *Theology,* p. 339, and W. Foerster, *TDNT,* 3:1088.

[10] Martin, p. 245.

[11] J. A. Motyer, *Philippian Studies: The Richness of Christ* (Chicago: Inter-Varsity Press, 1966), p. 83.

[12] J. B. Lightfoot, *Saint Paul's Epistle to the Philippians* (London: Macmillan, 1891), p. 114. See also Martin, p. 250.

[13] Lightfoot, p. 113.

[14] J. D. Douglas, ed., *The New Bible Dictionary* (Grand Rapids: Eerdmans, 1962), p. 863.

[15] Martin, p. 246. For a discussion of whether it is universal or ecclesiastical lordship to which Jesus attains, see Martin, pp. 249—55.

[16] Similar in meaning to James 2:19: 'The demons also believe, and shudder.' See Arndt-Gingrich-Danker, p. 277; Martin, pp. 263—64. Although the company of those so acclaiming Christ will certainly include hostile spirits, it is not necessary to understand it as exclusively so (as do Martin and many others, pp. 258—64). Arndt-Gingrich-Danker remark concerning *epigeiōn* ('of those on earth') that this class is 'not confined to human beings', implying that it does in fact include them. There is no compelling reason for excluding humans, redeemed or otherwise, from participation in this acknowledgement.

[17] For a discussion of the time of the universal confession, see Martin, pp. 266—70. The position adopted here is in agreement with that of Ladd, p. 416.

[18] For a fuller treatment of this matter see the appendix (p. 103), 'Consequences of the Hypostatic Union', by John Murray.

[19] Louis Berkhof, *Systematic Theology* (reprint ed., Edinburgh: Banner of Truth Trust, 1974), p. 406.

[20] The phrase is W. G. T. Shedd's, in *Dogmatic Theology*, 3 vols. (reprint ed., Grand Rapids: Zondervan, 1969), 2:353.

[21] Herman Hoeksema, *Reformed Dogmatics* (Grand Rapids: Reformed Free Publishing Association, 1966), p. 430.

[22] Shedd, 2:357.

[23] Hoeksema, p. 365. See also Herman Ridderbos, *Paul: An Outline of His Theology*, trans. John Richard De Witt (Grand Rapids: Eerdmans, 1975), pp. 560—62.

[24] Arndt-Gingrich-Danker, p. 681.

[25] Joseph Addison Alexander, *A Commentary on the Acts of the Apostles*, 2 vols. in 1 (reprint ed., London: Banner of Truth Trust, 1963), 1:82.

[26] Alexander, 1:82.

[27] Alexander, 1:82.

[28] Ladd, p. 336.

[29] The question whether we have here a pre-Pauline formula or an original Pauline passage does not affect the present discussion.

[30] This tendency is clearly evident in Robert H. Mounce, *The Essential Nature of New Testament Preaching* (Grand Rapids: Eerdmans, 1960), pp. 96—97.

[31] Ladd, p. 418.

[32] Cullmann, p. 235.

[33] John Murray, *The Epistle to the Romans,* 2 vols in 1, New International Commentary on the New Testament (Grand Rapids: Eerdmans, 1959, 1965).

[34] Murray, 1:9.

[35] Murray, 1:10.

[36] Murray, 1:7. For more recent support of the position adopted here, see C. E. B. Cranfield, *A Critical and Exegetical Commentary on the Epistle to the Romans,* 2 vols., International Critical Commentary (Edinburgh: T. & T. Clark, 1975, 1979), 1:61—65.

[37] Murray, 1:11. See Cullmann, p. 292.

[38] Murray, 1:12.

[39] Ladd, p. 418.

[40] Arndt-Gingrich-Danker, p. 193.

[41] Cf. Mark 2:10; John 17:2. The claim found in Matt. 11:27 should be understood as limited to the concerns of the immediate context, that is, the sovereign bestowal of salvation. See John A. Broadus, 'Commentary on the Gospel of Matthew', in Alvah Hovey, ed., *An American Commentary on the New Testament,* 7 vols. (Valley Forge: American Baptist Publication Society, 1886), 1:252.

[42] Arndt-Gingrich-Danker, p. 593. Compare the suggested meanings in the first two sections under *1.a.*

[43] Arndt-Gingrich-Danker, p. 278.

[44] *TDNT,* 3:1089.

[45] *TDNT,* 2:568.

[46] A. B. Bruce, 'The Synoptic Gospels', in W. Robertson Nicoll, ed., *The Expositor's Greek Testament,* 5 vols. (reprint ed., Grand Rapids: Eerdmans, 1967), 1:339.

[47] John Peter Lange, *Commentary on the Holy Scriptures: Critical, Doctrinal and Homiletical,* trans. and ed. Philip Schaff, 24 vols. in 12 (reprint ed., Grand Rapids: Zondervan, 1960), vol. 8, 'Matthew', pp. 561—62. Lange's whole note is worthy of attention.

[48] The word *oun* is omitted by some Greek manuscripts, but the weight of evidence favours its inclusion.

[49] 'It is on the basis of this mediatorial authority, in heaven and on earth, that the Saviour issues his commission to his followers.' Broadus, p. 592.

[50] F. F. Bruce, *The Epistle to the Ephesians* (Westwood, N.J.: Fleming H. Revell Co., 1961), p. 42. See also Arndt-Gingrich-Danker, pp. 174—75; *TDNT,* 2:37—40.

[51] Karl Braune, in Lange's *Commentary,* vol. 11, 'Ephesians', p. 61.

[52] Cullmann, p. 223.

[53] Arndt-Gingrich-Danker, p. 840.

[54] J. Armitage Robinson, *St. Paul's Epistle to the Ephesians* (London: James Clarke & Co., n.d.), p. 41.

[55] The meanings suggested by Arndt-Gingrich-Danker may be found on pages 112, 278, 208 and 461 respectively.

[56] T. K. Abbott, *A Critical and Exegetical Commentary on the Epistles to the Ephesians and to the Colossians,* International Critical Commentary (Edinburgh: T. & T. Clark, 1897), pp. 32—33.

[57] Robinson, p. 41.

[58] Cullmann, pp. 223—24.

[59] Robinson, p. 41.

[60] Brooke Foss Westcott, *Saint Paul's Epistle to the Ephesians* (reprint ed., Minneapolis: Klock & Klock Christian Publishers, 1978), p. 27.

[61] Arndt-Gingrich-Danker, p. 430.

[62] Bruce, p. 43.

[63] William Hendriksen, *Exposition of Ephesians,* New Testament Commentary (Grand Rapids: Baker, 1967), pp. 102–3.

[64] See Arndt-Gingrich-Danker, p. 597.

[65] See Murray, 2:182–83.

[66] For the meaning of this phrase see below.

[67] Arndt-Gingrich-Danker, p. 458.

[68] The contrary view is held by Ladd, p. 416.

[69] Murray, 2:181. Notice the genitive *tou kyriou* at the end of v. 8; NASB: 'We are the Lord's.'

[70] Murray, 2:183.

[71] Murray, 2:182.

[72] On this question Charles Hodge also writes, 'While the divine nature of Christ is the necessary *condition* of his exaltation, his mediatorial work is the immediate *ground* of the Theanthropos, God manifested in the flesh, being invested with this universal dominion.' (Emphasis mine.) Hodge, *Commentary on the Epistle to the Ephesians* (reprint ed., Old Tappan, N.J.: Fleming H. Revell Co., n.d.), p. 83.

## Ch. 3

[1] Arndt-Gingrich-Danker, p. 112.

[2] Cullmann, p. 220.

[3] Mounce, *The Essential Nature of New Testament Preaching.* Cf. C. H. Dodd, *The Apostolic Preaching and Its Developments,* 2nd ed. (New York: Harper, 1944).

[4] Mounce, p. 110.

[5] Mounce, p. 77.

[6] Mounce, pp. 88–109.

[7] Mounce, p. 108.

[8] Bruce, *Ephesians,* p. 41.

[9] Arndt-Gingrich-Danker, p. 431.

[10] The editors of modern Greek Testaments prefer the word order given here to that found in the NASB, which puts 'Christ' before 'Jesus'. The order does not affect the present discussion.

[11] Philip Edgcumbe Hughes, *Paul's Second Epistle to the Corinthians,* New International Commentary on the New Testament (Grand Rapids: Eerdmans, 1962), p. 131.

[12] Ladd, p. 339.

[13] Mounce, p. 94.

[14] Vernon H. Neufeld, *The Earliest Christian Confessions* (Grand Rapids: Eerdmans, 1963), pp. 62–63. The *hoti* of v. 9 should be translated 'that' (not 'because'), indicating the content of the message preached.

[15] Neufeld, p. 24.

[16] For more on the phrase 'our Lord', see below, pp.

[17] Mounce, p. 94. Neufeld argues convincingly that 'Jesus is the Christ' was the earliest confession, p. 142. Of course, lordship appears to be closely related to an exalted state of messiahship (Acts 2:36), so the two concepts are not entirely discontinuous.

[18] Neufeld, p. 51.

[19] Neufeld, p. 56. See also Cranfield, *Romans,* 2:527.

[20] *TDNT,* 5:200.

[21] *TDNT,* 5:209.

[22] Neufeld, p. 20. His study of the word is found in pp. 13–20.

[23] Murray, 2:55.

[24] Ladd, p. 416.

[25] While this is the necessary factual data which the confession acknowledges, the confession cannot be reduced to factual data alone, as Everett F. Harrison attempts to do in his work on Romans in *The Expositor's Bible Commentary* (10:112). Harrison's approach results in a mere intellectualism or 'historical faith' (an acknowledgement of factual data, not necessarily arising from spiritual regeneration). On 'historical faith' see Hoeksema, *Reformed Dogmatics,* p. 491.

[26] Ladd, p. 415. Charles Hodge's comment is also worth noting: 'This confession, therefore, includes in it an acknowledgement of Christ's universal sovereignty, and a sincere recognition of his authority over us.' *A Commentary on Romans* (reprint ed., London: Banner of Truth Trust, 1972), p. 341.

[27] Cranfield, 2:529. It is widely recognized that this is an implication of the title 'Lord' as applied to Jesus. 'Implicit in the recognition of the Lordship of Jesus is the acknowledgement of his essential divinity,' Ladd, p. 341. See also *TDNT*, 3:1089; Cullmann, pp. 234—35.

[28] Cranfield, 2:527.

[29] Arndt-Gingrich-Danker, p. 13.

[30] Neufeld, p. 63; Cullmann, pp. 218—20.

[31] Ladd, p. 415.

[32] See Neufeld, p. 65; Oscar Cullmann, *The Earliest Christian Confessions*, trans. J. K. S. Reid (London: Lutterworth Press, 1949), p. 32.

[33] Mounce, pp. 95—98; Neufeld, p. 51.

[34] Mounce, pp. 98—99; see also Neufeld, p. 51.

[35] Ladd, pp. 415—16. Cf. also Rom. 16:18, 'our Lord Christ'.

[36] Cullmann, *Christology*, p. 232. It should be noted that this confession occurs after the resurrection, and that it distinguishes between Jesus' identity as 'Lord' and as 'God'.

[37] For a discussion of this term, see Cullmann, *Christology*, pp. 208—15; Ladd, pp. 340—41; C. F. D. Moule, *The Origin of Christology* (Cambridge: Cambridge University Press, 1977), pp. 35—46.

[38] Cranfield, 2:529.

[39] Ladd, pp. 415—16.

[40] Harrison, 'Must Christ Be Lord?', p. 16.

[41] Ryrie, pp. 169—70.

[42] Arndt-Gingrich-Danker, p. 512.

[43] Ladd, p. 415.

[44] One of the rare instances of this use of *pisteuō* is in James 2:19, a verse which supports the point being made here. It is not a justifying 'faith' which the demons exercise.

[45] *TDNT*, 4:1003. Mounce's outline of the *kērygma* also notes the conjunction of the preaching of repentance and the lordship of Jesus; see above, p. 59.

[46] In John's preaching *metanoia* 'implies a change from within. This change must be demonstrated in the totality of a corres-

ponding life (Matt. 3:8), a life of love and righteousness in accordance with the will of God (Luke 3:10—14).' *TDNT*, 4:1001.

[47] 'The whole proclamation of Jesus, with its categorical demands for the sake of God's kingdom (the Sermon on the Mount, the sayings about discipleship) is a proclamation of *metanoia* even when the term is not used.' *TDNT*, 4:1002.

[48] As Lewis Sperry Chafer attempts to do with some passages, *Systematic Theology*, 3:375—76. It is worthy of note that in Acts the kingdom of God, as well as repentance, continues to be preached, even to Gentiles (Acts 8:12; 19:8; 20:25; 28:31). For a helpful treatment of the kingdom, see Ladd, pp. 34—210.

[49] As Ryrie attempts to do, pp. 175—76.

[50] John Murray, *Redemption Accomplished and Applied* (Grand Rapids: Eerdmans, 1955), p. 113. Chafer acknowledges this, 3:373—75.

[51] Ryrie, pp. 170—73.

[52] Harrison, 'Must Christ Be Lord?', p. 16.

[53] For a brief treatment of Ryrie's examples, see David C. Needham, *Birthright: Christian, Do You Know Who You Are?* (Portland, Oregon: Multnomah Press, 1979), p. 178. Needham's entire chapter, 'A New Master: The Lordship of Christ is Central' (pp. 167—84), is worthy of attention.

[54] Ryrie, pp. 182—91.

[55] Ryrie, p. 186. Ryrie's 'dedication' is based largely on his interpretation of Rom. 12:1. For a different understanding of this verse, see Cranfield, 2:598, especially note 4.

[56] Ryrie, p. 187.

[57] Harrison, 'Must Christ Be Lord?', p. 16.

[58] Ryrie, p. 170.

[59] Arndt-Gingrich-Danker, p. 458.

[60] For the interpretation of Romans 6, see Murray, *Romans*; and D. M. Lloyd-Jones, *Romans: An Exposition of Chapter 6* (London: Banner of Truth Trust, 1972).

[61] Arndt-Gingrich-Danker, pp. 742—43.

[62] 'Have You Made the Wonderful Discovery of the Spirit-Filled Life?' (Campus Crusade for Christ, 1966), p. 7.

[63] For a more detailed study of the 'carnal Christian' theory, see Ernest C. Reisinger, *What Should We Think of 'The Carnal Christian'?* (Edinburgh: Banner of Truth Trust, n.d.).

[64] Harrison, 'Must Christ Be Lord?', p. 14.

[65] Harrison, 'Must Christ Be Lord?', p. 16.

[66] Ryrie, pp. 173–76.

[67] Ryrie, pp. 178–79.

[68] Stott, 'Must Christ Be Lord?', p. 18.

[69] Stott, pp. 17, 18.

Ch. 4

[1] C. Peter Wagner, 'Who Found It?' *Eternity,* September 1977, p. 16.

[2] John W. Sanderson, *The Fruit of the Spirit* (Grand Rapids: Zondervan, 1972), p. 10.

[3] Sanderson, p. 10.

[4] Kenneth L. Gentry, 'The Great Option: A Study of the Lordship Controversy', *Baptist Reformation Review* 5 (Spring 1976): 78–79.

[5] Geoffrey B. Wilson, *Romans: A Digest of Reformed Comment*, rev. ed. (Edinburgh: Banner of Truth Trust, 1977), p. 178.

[6] Kenneth F. W. Prior, *The Way of Holiness* (London: Inter-Varsity Press, 1967), pp. 85–96.

Appendix

[1] From John Murray, *Collected Writings of John Murray,* vol. 2 (Edinburgh: Banner of Truth Trust, 1977), pp. 139–140.